THE
GAMER'S BAR

THE GAMER'S BAR
Cocktails and Mocktails for an Epic Game Night

Cassandra Reeder

Nadia Oxford

INSIGHT EDITIONS

SAN RAFAEL • LOS ANGELES • LONDON

CONTENTS

Introduction 6

Mixers 8

Tutorials and Inventory Items 10

RATED E FOR EVERYBODY.. 19

MULTIPLAYER MOCKTAILS.. 45

RETRO REVELS... 61

CHAOTIC GOOD COCKTAILS.. 91

RATED M FOR MATURE.. 119

CO-OP CONSUMABLES.. 147

Measurement Conversion Charts............................. 158

VIDEO GAMES ARE FINALLY OLD ENOUGH TO DRINK

Humans, like most animals living on earth, quickly learned there's a time to be sober, and a time to be soused. Animals stick to eating fermented fruit or, in actual documented cases of elephant behavior, rob farmers of corn liquor.

People aren't above drinking something that came out of a shack, but there is an appreciation for the art of the cocktail. There is an art to blending together a drink's ingredients until it yields the perfect color and texture. Imaginative folks even build drinks around media franchises and themes. Books. Movies. Video games. Yes, we're here to prove you can drink a video game.

We might live in an age where we're encouraged to liquefy a game's vision and pour it down our gob, but the relationship between video games and alcohol was tumultuous for a long time. Video games were initially regarded as a kid-exclusive pastime, which meant references to alcohol were censored in many North American game localizations in the '80s and '90s. That was especially true for games bound for Nintendo's systems, some of which went to impressive lengths to cover up characters' drinks, and the act of drinking itself.

Take the beloved NES boxing game Punch-Out!! for example. The Russian bruiser called Soda Popinski is seen chugging from a bottle in between bouts, and though Soda's (altered) name suggests otherwise, he ain't swigging pop. The story events of Final Fantasy VI (localized in North America as Final Fantasy III) for the SNES lead up to the literal end of the world, an understandably miserable event—but the survivors never touch a drop, at least not in the West. Even pub signs are altered to say café. Fair enough; not everyone likes to drink alcohol, and coffee is a fine substitute. But it's nice to give people the option while they're watching the world turn to poisoned ashes around them.

Even the first Mario Kart game keeps the winners' celebratory champagne out of their

mouths. In Japan, Princess Peach flushes beet red as she chugs like a champion, and Bowser just inhales his prize, alcoholic froth gathering around his mouth like a rabid dog's chops.

The Entertainment Software Ratings Board (ESRB) was established in 1994, and most game localizations backed off from the job of protecting kids' fragile little minds. If your kid buys a T-rated game he's not cool enough for, that's your lookout. However, game companies still do some self-editing when they deem it necessary. In the Game Boy phenomena Pokémon Red, Blue, and Green, you can't start your journey to stuff animals into balls until a drunk old man sobers up and staggers away from what is apparently the only viable path in Viridian City. In the North American version of Pokémon Red and Blue, the old man blocks your path because he hasn't had his coffee yet. ("Must be a Mondaaaay!") I get it in retrospect, little kids love Pokémon, and a hungover octogenarian isn't a kid-friendly mentor, but the coffee cover-up only confused me. If the old-timer wanted coffee that bad, why not get some instead of throwing a tantrum on Viridian City's single safe road?

Alcoholic drinks are represented more honestly in games today thanks to the enduring ESRB and a shift in attitudes toward games in general. We're long past the "kids' stuff" era, and we know for a fact that video games are enjoyed by almost every conceivable demographic. I think we're also more cognizant about responsible drinking. Alcohol is a great social lubricant for people who are socially awkward on a terminal level, and it's lovely to enjoy a favorite game with a drink (maybe one of the drinks in this very book!) at your side. But always be aware of your limits. Rest assured this book has a plethora of virgin options. Virgin drinks—not the "sacrifice to a sea god" type of virgin.

MIXERS

You know how in some games you add a purple flower and an entire wheel of cheese to a cauldron and out pops a mana potion? This is like that, only logical. Mixers are the building blocks of cocktails. Sometimes they're all that stands between you and chugging booze straight from the bottle. To sweeten things up, we've got simple syrup (sugar water), grenadine (sugar water but pomegranate flavored), and blue syrup, also known as blue curaçao syrup, because we all deserve bright blue drinks too. And finally, to help boost the flavor of citrus-forward drinks, we've got bartender's saline, a simple salt solution.

SIMPLE SYRUP

- » 1 cup water
- » 1 cup granulated sugar

DIRECTIONS:

1. In a small saucepan, combine the water and sugar.
2. Heat the water and sugar over medium heat until simmering, stirring frequently, until the sugar has fully dissolved.
3. Cover and let simmer for 3 to 5 minutes.
4. Allow the syrup to cool, then transfer it to a sealable glass container.
5. Store in the refrigerator for up to 4 weeks.

GRENADINE

- » 1 cup pomegranate juice
- » 2 teaspoons lemon juice
- » 1 cup granulated sugar
- » 2 or 3 dashes orange flower water (optional)

DIRECTIONS:

1. In a medium saucepan, combine the pomegranate juice, lemon juice, and sugar.
2. Bring the mixture to a simmer over medium heat, stirring frequently. Reduce the heat to low and cover. Simmer on low for 10 to 15 minutes, stirring occasionally.
3. Allow the mixture to cool, then pour it into a small sealable jar or glass bottle.
4. Stir in the orange flower water (if using) and seal the container. Give it a couple shakes.
5. Let cool before using. Store in the refrigerator for up to 4 weeks.

BLUE SYRUP

» 3 navel oranges
» 1½ cups granulated sugar
» 1½ cups water
» 1 tablespoon lemon juice
» 2 or 3 whole cloves (optional)
» 2 to 4 drops orange bitters (optional)
» 1 teaspoon blue food coloring (amount needed may vary)

DIRECTIONS:

1. Peel the oranges using a vegetable peeler or a hand grater.
2. Put the sugar and orange peels in a medium saucepan. Rub the sugar into the peel until the peels release some oil and become fragrant.
3. Add the water, lemon juice, and cloves (if using) to the saucepan and stir.
4. Bring to a simmer over medium heat. Let simmer for 2 to 3 minutes until the sugar has dissolved.
5. Remove the saucepan from the heat and let the peels steep for 45 minutes to an hour.
6. Pour through a fine-mesh strainer into an airtight glass storage container, such as a mason jar.
7. Stir in the orange bitters to taste (if using).
8. Stir in the blue food coloring until the syrup is a deep, dark blue color.
9. Store in the refrigerator for up to 1 month.

SALINE

» 1 tablespoon sea salt
» ⅓ cup warm purified water

DIRECTIONS:

1. In a small bowl, combine the salt and warm water.
2. Stir until the salt has fully dissolved.
3. Use a funnel to transfer to a storage container, ideally 1 or 2 dropper bottles.
4. Give the bottle a few quick shakes.
5. Store in a cool, dark place indefinitely.

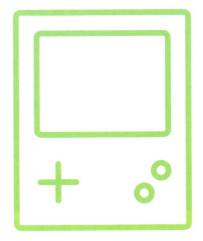

TUTORIALS AND INVENTORY ITEMS

Were you the kind of person who actually read the tutorial booklets, back when that was a thing? If so, then this section is for you, dear reader. Here, we'll tell you all the moves and mechanics necessary for making fantastic drinks. And you don't even have to press a single button to skip it!

JIGGERS AND MEASUREMENTS

What is a jigger?

A jigger is a tool used to measure alcohol accurately and consistently. A standard jigger features two cups, one larger and one smaller, joined in an hourglass shape. The larger cup typically holds 1.5 ounces, or one "jigger." The smaller cup typically holds 0.75 ounces, or one-half jigger, also known as a "pony" shot. There is some variation in cup size between the different styles of jiggers, so make sure you know the measurements of your individual jigger.

Alternatives

Though using a jigger is highly recommended, you can get away with using other common measuring tools. The key is consistency: You don't want to eyeball it unless you have a lot of experience, but some measuring spoons will work just fine!

- » 3 ounces or a "double" shot = 6 tablespoons
- » 2 ounces = ¼ cup or 4 tablespoons
- » 1.5 ounces or 1 jigger = 3 tablespoons
- » 1 ounce or 1 shot = 2 tablespoons
- » 0.75 ounce or a "pony" shot = 1½ tablespoons
- » 0.5 ounces = 1 tablespoon
- » 0.25 ounce = ½ tablespoon
- » 1 barspoon = 1 teaspoon

ICE

Why ice type matters

The type of ice used in cocktails can change the texture, dilution, and overall flavor of a drink. Here are four of the most common types of ice and how they will impact your cocktail.

Standard

Standard-size ice cubes are about 1 inch or 1.25 inches. This is the ice that comes in most ice trays and ice makers. These versatile ice cubes won't melt too fast or too slow and will work well in most cocktails. When using standard ice in the serving glass, add the ice to fill after the drink has been poured, unless the drink is layered, or the drink instructions say otherwise.

Crushed

Crushed ice is perfect for drinks that could use a little extra dilution. If you don't have an ice machine that makes crushed ice, you can always make it yourself. Just toss your standard ice cubes in a blender with a little water, pulse, and strain any of the excess water before adding the ice to your glass. Generally, crushed ice should mostly fill the entire serving glass. Using too little crushed ice will cause too much dilution because the ice will melt too quickly.

Large
Large ice cubes are typically 2 inches or larger and are best used for spirit-forward drinks. Because of the large surface area, they will dilute the drink much more slowly than standard ice cubes.

Shaped
Ice spheres are a popular choice thanks to their slow melt rate and attractive appearance, doubling as a stunning garnish. For highball cocktails (a family of mixed drinks), the long, sleek collins spears are an ideal choice, although standard ice works fine. There are also fun shapes like roses, skulls, or diamonds, which add a little extra personality to any drink.

GLASSWARE
Glassware plays a big role in both presentation and flavor. Each drink recipe in this book will include suggestions for which serving vessel to use to maximize your presentation.

Cocktail glasses, martini glasses, and coupes
The cocktail glass is an inverted cone, its large mouth allowing drinkers to take in aroma of the drink. The martini glass makes for a classic, stylish presentation, and its long stem prevents the drinker's body heat from warming the drink. Although originally meant to serve champagne, coupes have become a popular alternative to the martini glass.

Collins and highball
These tall and slender glasses are ideal for fizzy drinks; their shape keeps drinks carbonated longer.

Shot glasses
Shot glasses only contain a couple ounces of liquid. Drinks served in a shot glass are typically meant to be taken in one swig.

Rocks and lowballs
Primarily used for serving spirit-forward drinks, these glasses are short and have a thick bottom.

Margarita glasses
A variation on the coupe, the margarita glass's large rim hosts plenty of surface area, making it ideal for cocktails with a flavored rim.

Wine and beer glasses
Wineglasses are typically used for serving wine, which makes them great for wine-based cocktails like sangria. Similarly, beer glasses are a fantastic choice for drinks that are mixed with beer, such as shandies.

Specialty
Sometimes a special drink requires a special glass. For instance, copper mugs are used for serving mules because the metal keeps the drink cold!

GARNISHING

What is a cocktail garnish?
A cocktail garnish is an ornamental item added to a drink, which adds visual appeal to the beverage. As with ice and glassware, garnishes can also have flavor-enhancing qualities.

Why garnish?
Although garnishing is optional, garnishes can really enhance the drinking experience. Cherries and citrus fruits are popular choices as a quick and easy way to add sweetness, aroma, and color. A sprig of fresh mint adds a strong aromatic element as well as a pop of bright green color. Salt rims not only look good, they intensify the flavor of citrus-forward drinks like margaritas. In this book, we will use garnishes to create a fun visual that is reminiscent of a video game character, story, or item.

How to garnish
Garnishing is a great opportunity to add your personality to a drink; there is no right or wrong way to do it. Arrange your garnishes in whatever way makes you happy!

Tips
When using a citrus peel or a citrus twist, make sure to remove as much of the pith (the white part) of the peel as possible. The garnish will not only look better, but the pith can impart a bitter flavor over time.

SHAKING

What is shaking a cocktail?
Shaking a cocktail is the act of adding ingredients to a cocktail shaker (or other makeshift vessel), with or without ice, and agitating the ingredients. This is usually done with a cocktail shaker, but in a pinch, you can use a stainless-steel travel mug.

Why shake?
Shaking a cocktail achieves a few things: it chills, aerates, and dilutes the drink. We usually think of dilution as a bad thing when it comes to drinking, but when done correctly, it actually helps the ingredients blend together, creating a smoother and more cohesive cocktail. And shaking is absolutely crucial in drinks that contain egg whites, creating a velvety mouthfeel and a smooth foam layer that rests on top of the drink.

How to shake a cocktail
After adding the ingredients, place one hand on the bottom of the shaker and one on top of the lid. Make sure your grip is firm to ensure the shaker stays intact while shaking. Shake vigorously in a horizontal motion over your shoulder. The time you spend shaking will depend on the specific cocktail, but most of the time, it will be 10 to 15 seconds or until the shaker frosts up.

Dry shaking
Most of the time, cocktails are shaken with ice to chill and dilute the drink, also called "wet shaking." However, cocktails that include egg whites will first need to be shaken without ice, or "dry shaking." This results in a rich, frothy texture when the egg whites react to the citrus in the drink and the agitation from the shaking.

Tips
You only want to use standard and/or large ice cubes in the cocktail shaker, never crushed ice, because it will melt too quickly and cause the drink to become watery. Too much dilution IS a bad thing.

STIRRING

What is stirring a cocktail?
Not many drinks in this book require stirring, but for those that do, here is a quick guide! Stirring is just what it sounds like. In the case of cocktails, it's an alternative to shaking that works better for certain drinks. Usually, when a cocktail is "stirred," it means the ingredients were stirred with ice in a separate glass, called a mixing glass, and then strained into the serving glass. A mixing glass doesn't have to be anything special; it just needs to have a wide enough opening so that you can give the drink a decent stir. A rocks glass will work fine, in most cases.

Why stir?
A gentler method than shaking, stirring allows the drink to be chilled but does not change the texture or appearance of the drink. Though there are always exceptions, a common rule is that drinks that contain mostly or entirely spirits, without any fruit juices, should be stirred.

How to stir a cocktail
Ideally, you should chill the mixing glass first. This can be done by placing the glass in the freezer for 10 to 15 minutes or by adding ice water to the glass, stirring, and discarding the ice water. Add the drink ingredients and fill the glass two-thirds full with standard ice. Place a spoon (ideally a barspoon) into the mixing glass so the back of the spoon sits against the edge of the glass. Move the spoon around the edge of the glass to rotate the ice. Do this for 20 to 30 seconds until the ingredients are well chilled, then strain the liquid into a serving glass.

Tips
Try to be as gentle as possible when stirring a drink. Unlike shaking, the idea of stirring is to cause as little agitation as possible while chilling the drink.

BUILDING

What is building a cocktail?
Building essentially means adding the drink ingredients directly to the serving glass in a specific order.

Why build?
Usually, if a drink contains bubbles or layers, it's better to build. Sometimes you'll want to shake the individual layers first, but after the carbonated ingredients have been added to the drink, you don't want to mess with it too much, lest it become flat.

How to build
Building a drink varies from drink to drink, so there's no standard way to do it; you will want to follow the order given in the individual recipe. Generally, for drinks with carbonated ingredients, the non-carbonated ingredients go in first, then the carbonated ingredients are added to fill (meaning to the top). For layered drinks, typically the layers with the most density—usually the sweetest and least alcoholic ingredients—will go in first. More on layering later!

Tips
Building is the simplest of the cocktail-making techniques, but there can be pitfalls. You must be mindful of the order in which the ingredients are added to the drink, as adding them in the wrong order could negatively affect it.

LAYERING

Why layer?
Layering ingredients can add visual appeal to a drink and create a more colorful presentation. A popular example is a sunrise cocktail, which uses crème de cassis or grenadine and fruit juices to make a drink that is reminiscent of the rising sun.

How to layer
The process of layering is easier than it seems. The basic rule is that the heaviest liquids need to be at the bottom. The heaviest liquids also tend to be the sweetest or most sugar dense. Though there are some exceptions depending on the ingredient, cocktail layers usually work out like this:

Base layer: Syrups
Second layer: Liqueurs
Third layer: Juices or dairy
Fourth layer: Spirits
Fifth layer: Foam (from egg whites or aquafaba) or whipped cream

How to layer
The easiest trick for achieving distinct layers is by using a spoon. Ideally, you would use a barspoon, but any small spoon will work. Holding the spoon directly over the base layer, slowly pour the next layer over the spoon, letting it overflow. This should result in the next layer floating on top of the previous layer, creating a visual contrast. Continue until you have created all your layers.

Tips
Despite the common instruction to use the back of the spoon, it doesn't tend to make much difference in practice. With smaller cups, such as a shot glass, it is actually much easier to hold the spoon facing upward.

RIMMING

Some recipes in this cocktail book call for the serving glass to be rimmed. Rimming a glass is easy, takes less than a minute, and greatly enhances the flavor and appearance of a drink. Here is a general guideline to help. Note: Most recipes will only call for a liquid and a rimmer. Additional flavoring and food coloring are less common and completely optional.

- » 1 to 2 tablespoons liquid (such as juice or syrup)
- » 1 to 2 tablespoons rimmer (such as salt or sugar)
- » 1 teaspoon other flavorings (such as citrus zest or spices) (optional)
- » 1 to 2 drops food coloring (optional)

Rimming directions:
1. Pour the liquid into a small shallow bowl.
2. In a separate small shallow bowl, stir together the rimmer, flavorings (if using), and food coloring (if using).
3. Turn the serving glass upside down and dip the rim of the glass into the liquid.
4. Dip the moistened rim of the glass into the shallow bowl with the rimmer mixture.
5. Rotate the glass so that the rimmer mixture sticks to the moistened rim.
6. Set the glass aside while you prepare the drink.

MUDDLING

What is muddling?
Muddling is the act of gently smashing ingredients like herbs, fruits, and spices so that they release their essence into a drink. This is typically done with a tool called a muddler, but you can improvise if necessary!

Why muddle?
Muddling helps release the flavors of the herbs or fruits being used.

How to muddle
The easiest way is using a specifically designed tool called a "muddler." However, one can use any long, blunt instrument, such as the handle of a wooden spoon, to muddle. You may just have to work slightly harder. Here are the steps to create a proper muddle:

1. Put the ingredients into a glass with a study base or a cocktail shaker.
2. Gently but firmly push down and twist the muddler at the same time.
3. Repeat this motion five or six times until the ingredients are fragrant and lightly smashed.

Tips
Be careful not to over-muddle or press too hard. This can damage and bruise your ingredients, causing unpleasant flavors for certain herbs like mint. It can also break a glass and/or hurt your hands.

SUBSTITUTIONS

Whether you have dietary restrictions, food allergies, or just really don't like rum: We've got you. Here are some suggestions for easy swaps and seamless substitutions that will help you customize your drinking experience.

Bourbon, whiskey, and scotch:
Alcoholic
» Brandy or cognac
» Dark/aged rum

Nonalcoholic
» 1:1 commercial substitutes (zero-proof or nonalcoholic bourbon or whiskey)
» 1:1 strongly brewed barley tea, bourbon black tea, or rooibos
» 1:1 lapsang souchong tea (for scotch only)

Brandy and cognac
Alcoholic
» Bourbon or whiskey
» Dark/aged rum

Nonalcoholic
» 1:1 commercial substitutes (zero-proof or nonalcoholic brandies)
» Combine 1 tablespoon brandy extract with ½ cup apple juice. Use an equal (1:1) amount of this mixture in place of however much brandy the recipe calls for.
» 1:1 apple juice

Champagne and sparkling wine:
» 1:1 sparkling apple cider (for champagne or prosecco)
» 1:1 sparkling cran-apple juice (for sparkling rosé)

Cream and milk:
- Cream and half-and-half
- Cashew cream
- Full-fat coconut milk
- Commercial unflavored vegan and/or plant-based creams
- Milk
- Coconut milk
- Oat milk
- Almond milk
- Soy milk
- Sweetened condensed milk
- Sweetened condensed coconut milk
- Sweetened condensed oat milk
- Evaporated milk
- Evaporated coconut milk
- Evaporated oat milk

Gin:
Alcoholic
- Genever
- Vodka

Nonalcoholic
- Commercial substitutes (zero-proof or nonalcoholic gin)
- 1:1 juniper tea or juniper-infused water
- Floral herbal teas
- Kombucha (herbal flavors)

Egg whites:
- 3 tablespoons aquafaba (chickpea water)
- Commercial cocktail foamers (amount will vary by brand)

Liqueurs:
Fruit liqueurs
- Syrups: Many fruit liqueurs can be substituted with similarly flavored syrups. For instance, raspberry liqueur can be substituted with raspberry syrup and coconut rum with coconut syrup. Depending on the potency of the syrup, you may need to use slightly less syrup than liqueur. You may also need to use food coloring to achieve the same bright colors. For instance, if your melon syrup is clear, you may want to add some green food coloring.
- Shrubs, cordials, or other commercial mixers

Cream liqueurs
- Flavored coffee creamers: Irish cream-flavored coffee creamer can usually be used instead of Irish cream.
- Syrups: Chocolate or white chocolate syrup can be used instead of chocolate or white chocolate liqueur.

Herbal liqueurs
- Syrups: In most cases, peppermint syrup works just as well as peppermint liqueur, or violet syrup instead of crème de violet, etc.
- Sweetened herbal teas: Sweetened anise tea can be used instead of anise-based liqueurs like absinthe.
- Shrubs, cordials, or other commercial mixers: Elderflower cordial is an excellent substitute for elderflower liqueur.

Nut liqueurs
- Syrups: Use almond, orgeat, or amoretti syrup in place of amaretto liqueur, or hazelnut syrup instead of hazelnut liqueur, etc.

Red wine:
- 1:1 pomegranate juice
- 1:1 cranberry juice

Rum:
Alcoholic
- Cachaça
- Cognac or bourbon (for dark rum)
- Vodka or pisco (for white rum)

Nonalcoholic
- 1:1 commercial substitutes (zero-proof or nonalcoholic rums)
- 1 tablespoon rum extract and ½ cup apple and/or pineapple juice. Use an equal (1:1) amount of this mixture in place of however much rum the recipe calls for.
- 1:1 sugarcane juice
- 1:1 coconut water

Tequila and mezcal:
Alcoholic
- Rum
- Smoked rum or scotch (for mezcal only)

Nonalcoholic
For tequila:
- 1:1 commercial substitutes (zero-proof or nonalcoholic tequila)
- Equal parts lime juice, agave syrup, and water
- Kombucha (citrus and/or spiced flavors)

For mezcal:
- Commercial substitutes (zero-proof or nonalcoholic mezcal)
- Equal parts lime juice, agave syrup, and water plus 1 drop of liquid smoke
- 1:1 lapsang souchong tea

Vodka:
Alcoholic
- Gin
- White rum

Nonalcoholic
- 1:1 commercial substitutes (zero-proof or nonalcoholic vodka)
- ½ teaspoon apple cider vinegar plus 1 ounce water (use this per 1 ounce of vodka in the recipe)
- 1:1 water
- 1:1 kombucha (neutral or citrus flavors)

White Wine:
- 1:1 white grape juice
- 1:1 white cranberry juice

- 21   The 1Up
- 22   Cucco for Lon Lon Milk
- 25   The Hesitant Maverick Hunter
- 26   The Highwind
- 29   Kirby's Dreamland
- 30   Meowlotov Cocktail
- 33   The Pacifist Run
- 34   Princess Peach
- 37   Rainbow Road
- 38   The Speedy Blue Hedgehog
- 41   Super Mar . . . garita
- 42   WarioPear: Shake It!

THE 1UP

>>>>>>>>>>>>>>>>>>

SERVING VESSEL: Rocks, sour, or coupe
SERVES: 1

In the *Super Mario* series, bopping a block and finding a green-capped mushroom inside rewards you with another life. "Life" might not be your preferred nomenclature. You might say "extra man," or "another try," or "a new guy." Whatever you call this gift, we all understand it answers to the one true name: the 1Up.

Much has been philosophized about the nature of the 1Up. Seriously, people have existential crises when they start wondering how Mario perceives death and rebirth compared to the rest of us. Does it hurt to die? Or is he not really dead until his last 1Up is spent? How does he come back? Does he emerge fully grown from the womb? All right, let's pump the brakes here. Make yourself a drink and go play some *Duck Hunt*.

FOR THE DRINK:

- ½ lime (pick a nice-looking bright green one)
- 2 tablespoons white chocolate sauce
- 4 ounces (carton, not canned) coconut milk or almond milk*
- ½ tablespoon matcha powder
- ½ teaspoon pandan extract*

FOR THE GARNISH:

- Peel of the squeezed lime half
- 4 or 5 white chocolate chips or white royal icing

MODIFICATIONS:

- **Ultra Shroom (alcoholic):** Add 1.5 ounces of vodka and swap 1 tablespoon of white chocolate syrup with 1 ounce of white chocolate liqueur.

*You can find pandan extract online or at most Asian grocery stores. If you can't find it, use 1 or 2 drops each of vanilla extract and green food coloring.

*Canned coconut milk is made for cooking and tends to separate when chilled, whereas carton coconut milk often contains less fat and thickeners that prevent separation.

DIRECTIONS:

1. Juice the lime half and set the juice aside. Scoop the remaining flesh from the inside of the lime.
2. Use a sharp paring knife to cut four or five holes around the outside of the lime half. Skewer the lime half from the top so it is facing down like a mushroom cap, then stick the white chocolate chips in the holes. Alternatively, make the white mushroom spots with white royal icing. Set this aside while you make the drink.
3. In a mixing glass, combine the squeezed lime juice, chocolate sauce, coconut milk, matcha powder, and pandan extract.
4. Use a milk frother and mix until frothy. If you don't have a milk frother, whisk vigorously until well mixed.
5. Transfer the drink to the serving glass.
6. Add standard ice to taste.
7. Garnish the drink with the lime "mushroom" cap.

SERVING VESSEL:
Glass bottle or a tall glass
SERVES: 1

CUCCO FOR LON LON MILK

<<<<<<<<<<<<<<<<<

Hyrule's Lon Lon Ranch has everything an adventurer needs to outfit themselves and enjoy a little peace and quiet before hitting the road again. The cows' gentle lows soothe the soul, and the friendly horses approach you for a song. Lon Lon's delicious milk is available for purchase, but word has it the cows will give up their creamy bounty if you whip out your ocarina.

Lon Lon's cuccos, though? Don't even look at them. They appear to be chickens, but they're not chickens; they're legions of demons who took over the body of every chicken in Hyrule because they couldn't find any pigs. All right, that's a bit dramatic, but cuccos are obviously descendant from some raptor-like creature that evolved on Hyrule's plains and never forgot the sweet taste of blood. Don't let them catch you drinking the yolks of their unrealized children or there's going to be some friction.

· ·

FOR THE DRINK:
- » 2 ounces sweetened condensed milk
- » 1 egg yolk
- » 1 teaspoon vanilla extract
- » ¼ teaspoon ground cinnamon
- » 1 or 2 drops orange flower water (optional)
- » 3 to 4 ounces club soda, chilled

FOR THE GARNISH:
- » Pinch ground cinnamon and/or nutmeg (optional)

MODIFICATIONS:
- » **Talon's Secret (alcoholic):** Add 1.5 ounces of gin or vanilla vodka and 0.5 ounce cream of liqueur (such as Irish cream or horchata liqueur) along with the club soda.
- » **Weird Egg:** Replace the egg yolk with 0.75 ounce of evaporated milk.

DIRECTIONS:
1. In a mixing glass, whisk the condensed milk, egg yolk, vanilla, ground cinnamon, and orange flower water (if using) until well combined.
2. Strain into a glass bottle. You may need to use a funnel depending on the bottle's opening size.
3. Top with club soda. Use a straw or chopstick to stir.

THE HESITANT MAVERICK HUNTER

>>>>>>>>>>>>>>>>>

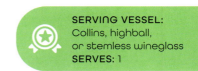

SERVING VESSEL:
Collins, highball,
or stemless wineglass
SERVES: 1

In *Mega Man X*, main character X is the final work of genius roboticist Dr. Thomas Light. Can he chug cocktails? He probably wishes he could. X is a lover of peace, but his very existence sparked a bloody war between humans and Reploids. Anyone else in the same life circumstances, human or robot, would surely need a drink after a hard day of painting the walls of some alley with synthetic blood.

The Hesitant Maverick Hunter acknowledges X's burden with its azure hue and sweet-and-sour kick. The cherry garnish imitates the red jewel in X's helmet. Shine on, young Hunter. Find your peace.

FOR THE DRINK:
- 1 ounce Blue Syrup (page 9)
- 2 ounces lemonade
- 0.25 ounce lime juice
- 3 or 4 drops orange bitters (optional)
- 2 to 3 ounces lemon-lime soda, chilled

FOR THE GARNISH:
- 1 red maraschino cherry

MODIFICATIONS:
- **Why Was I Programmed to Feel Pain? (alcoholic):** Substitute 1 ounce of lemonade with 1.5 ounces of citron vodka and swap the syrup for blue curaçao liqueur.

DIRECTIONS
1. In a cocktail shaker filled with ice, add the blue curaçao syrup, lemonade, lime juice, and bitters (if using).
2. Shake for 10 to 15 seconds until well chilled.
3. Strain into a tall serving glass.
4. Add the lemon-lime soda to fill.
5. Garnish with a skewered maraschino cherry.

SERVING VESSEL: Hurricane, can-shaped glass, or mason jar
SERVES: 1

THE HIGHWIND

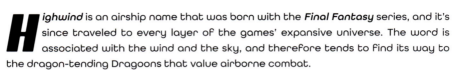

Highwind is an airship name that was born with the *Final Fantasy* series, and it's since traveled to every layer of the games' expansive universe. The word is associated with the wind and the sky, and therefore tends to find its way to the dragon-tending Dragoons that value airborne combat.

Characters bearing the Highwind surname are often like rescue dogs: They have wonderful hearts, but they also have big problems. Ricard Highwind of *Final Fantasy II* has no sense of self-preservation. Kain Highwind of *Final Fantasy IV* covets his best friend's station in life—and his woman. Cid Highwind of *Final Fantasy VII* . . . er, well, he has a list of issues. He's determined to be a good host, however foul-mouthed, so when the man offers you strange blue tea, you sit your ass down and drink it. Then you get drunk and hit a Shinra manager with a truck.

FOR THE BLUE TEA:
» 2 tablespoons butterfly pea flower tea
» 8 ounces boiling water

FOR THE DRINK:
» 6 to 8 ounces blue tea, chilled
» 2 to 3 ounces coconut milk (carton, not canned)
» 1 ounce cream of coconut syrup or sweetened condensed milk

FOR THE GARNISH:
» Marshmallow cream

DIRECTIONS:
1. To make the tea, in a glass mug or jar, combine the butterfly pea flower tea and hot water. Let it steep for 5 to 10 minutes until a deep blue color, then strain out the flowers with a fine-mesh strainer. Allow the tea to cool to room temperature or place it in the fridge to chill. Alternatively, you can steep the tea in room-temperature water for 1 to 2 hours.
2. Spread some dollops of marshmallow cream on the sides of the serving glass to create little "clouds."
3. In a separate container, use a milk frother to froth the coconut cream and the cream of coconut or sweetened condensed milk, if desired. Or just use a whisk to mix them together until the syrup is well incorporated.
4. Add standard ice to the serving glass until two-thirds full.
5. Add the blue tea and sweetened coconut milk to the serving glass and stir to combine until the color turns a lovely sky-blue color.
6. Drink your goddamn tea!

KIRBY'S DREAMLAND

>>>>>>>>>>>>>>>>>

SERVING VESSEL:
Milkshake glass, mason jar, or can-shaped glass
SERVES: 1

An Elder God dwells in Nintendo's universe, and his name is Kirby. The adorable pink puff has a knack for tumbling into adventures that start in lands made of dreams and clouds, only to invariably face off against a biblically accurate angel, and/or something that resembles Tetsuo at the end of *Akira* crossed with a Hello Kitty character.

We don't know what's going on with Kirby. We'll never know. We're not **meant** to know. But we can't shake the feeling he's protecting us all against something that lives at the coldest, darkest edge of Nintendo's multiverse, something that will induce madness if we look at it. Show your thanks to our savior by offering up this pink ice-cream dream. Then slowly step away from the altar.

FOR THE DRINK:

- 2 or 3 pieces canned jackfruit or peaches, plus 1 teaspoon liquid
- 2 tablespoons nata de coco, plus 1 teaspoon liquid
- 2 tablespoons strawberry popping boba, plus 1 teaspoon liquid
- 2 ounces brewed strawberry or passion tea, chilled (or use another pink fruity tea)
- 3 ounces milk
- 0.5 ounce dragon fruit syrup (sub strawberry syrup or grenadine)
- 1 or 2 drops red or pink food coloring (optional, for more vivid color)

FOR THE GARNISH:

- 1 slice star fruit, for garnish
- 1 scoop strawberry ice cream
- 1 boba straw

DIRECTIONS:

1. Use a sharp knife to cut up the jackfruit and nata de coco into pieces small enough to fit through a boba straw.
2. In a milkshake or hurricane glass, combine the chopped jackfruit, nata de coco, and strawberry boba. Add about a teaspoon of each syrup to the fruit.
3. Add crushed ice to fill. Add the milk, syrup, and tea. Give everything a stir until well combined and uniform in color. If the pink color is too pale for your liking, stir in 1 or 2 drops of pink or red food coloring.
4. Top with a scoop of strawberry ice cream and garnish with a star fruit slice.
5. Drink with a wide straw, like those made for boba tea, and suck up the fruit on the bottom like Kirby.

SERVING VESSEL:
Cocktail glass
SERVES: 1

MEOWLOTOV COCKTAIL

<<<<<<<<<<<<<<<<

Monster hunters who stalk the mightiest prey and live to tell the tale know that it's not the weapon that decides your victory—it's the fearless partner who will literally throw themselves into a Rathalos's mouth to protect you.

Humans and Felynes are fast friends and allies, as both races have traits that complement each other on the hunting grounds. Humans wield diverse weapons that are capable of targeting even the fiercest wyvern's weakness, whereas Felynes use their uncanny kitty reflexes to nip at the heels of prey that's much, much bigger than they are. And when the monster inevitably falls, when it's butchered for parts and hauled away, human and Felyne alike will toast their friendship with drinks in hand. And in paw.

TO MAKE THE DRINK:

- 1 or 2 bird's-eye chile peppers, chopped (but reserve the pointy tips)
- 1 teaspoon sakura (cherry blossom) powder
- 0.5 ounce Grenadine (page 8)
- 2 ounces lychee juice (can be from canned lychees)
- 2 to 3 ounces seltzer water

FOR THE GARNISH:

- 1 lychee
- 2 bird's-eye chiles (just the ends)
- 1 cocktail skewer

MODIFICATIONS:

- **Poogie's Pink Delight (alcoholic):** Add 1.5 ounces of cherry blossom gin or another Japanese gin. Regular gin is also fine in a pinch. Choose one that has a strong botanical or floral aroma.

DIRECTIONS:

1. First, prepare the garnish. Use a knife to poke two holes into a peeled lychee. Inset the tips of two bird's-eye chiles into the holes so that they look like cat ears. Skewer with a cocktail skewer. Set aside.
2. In a cocktail shaker, gently muddle the chopped chile peppers.
3. Fill the cocktail shaker with standard ice.
4. Add the sakura powder, grenadine, and lychee juice to the shaker.
5. Shake for 10 to 15 seconds until well chilled.
6. Strain into the serving glass.
7. Add seltzer to fill.
8. Garnish with the cat lychee.

THE PACIFIST RUN

>>>>>>>>>>>>>>>>>>

SERVING VESSEL: Glass mug or other hot drink vessel
SERVES: 1

For decades, popular anthropologists preached that humans are inherently violent creatures who killed and conquered their Neanderthal cousins and other early hominid tribes. We now know that's not exactly the case. No doubt we killed each other in our struggle for resources, and no question humans are capable of inflicting great pain on themselves and others. But we're just as capable, if not more capable, of great empathy.

That's a fancy way of saying our Ice Age precursors were more keen on making love than war, and that still holds. Blessed are the video games that let us take a gentler route to the final goal. There's a time to fight and drink whiskey, and there's a time to chill and drink something sweet and velvety.

FOR THE DRINK:
- 1 cup full-fat oat milk or whole milk
- 1 tablespoon loose-leaf chamomile tea or 1 chamomile tea bag
- 1 or 2 cinnamon sticks
- 2 or 3 whole cloves
- 1 teaspoon vanilla extract
- 1 tablespoon butterscotch syrup

FOR THE GARNISH:
- Ground cinnamon
- Edible flower

MODIFICATIONS:
- **No Mercy Route (alcoholic):** Add 1.5 ounces of brandy or spiced rum. Replace the butterscotch syrup with 0.75 ounce butterscotch schnapps (or to taste). Add these directly to the serving glass before adding the milk mixture.

DIRECTIONS:
1. In a small saucepan, bring the milk, chamomile, cinnamon sticks, cloves, and vanilla to a low simmer over low heat. Allow to simmer for 4 to 5 minutes.
2. Turn off the heat, cover, and continue to steep for another 5 minutes.
3. Strain through a fine-mesh strainer into the serving glass. Discard the tea and cloves. Save the cinnamon sticks for garnish, if you'd like.
4. Stir in the butterscotch syrup to taste.
5. Sprinkle ground cinnamon on top of the drink. Garnish with cinnamon sticks and edible flowers.

SERVING VESSEL:
Milkshake glass or hurricane
SERVES: 1 to 2

PRINCESS PEACH

<<<<<<<<<<<<<<<<

Dear Mario: It's me, Toad. Please come to the castle. Princess Peach baked a cake for you, and we need you to check it out. See, she took the cake mix and, uh, stuffed it in a glass with some ice cream? And she topped it with a yogurt swirl that has a crown on top of it. I guess that's so we don't forget she's the princess. Is she scared we're going to forget she's the princess? I don't know if I've seen her sleep over the past five days.

I hope you get this letter, Mario. I pray you're not out of town doing that weird paper thing again. Help us.

· ·

FOR THE DRINK:
- 1 cup milk
- 2 scoops vanilla ice cream
- ½ cup peach yogurt
- ½ cup frozen peaches
- ¼ cup vanilla cake mix
- 1 to 2 tablespoons Grenadine (page 8)
- ½ cup ice
- 1 or 2 drops red or pink food coloring (optional, for a brighter pink)

FOR THE GARNISH:
- Whipped cream
- Gold sprinkles
- 1 lemon peel, cut into a crown shape or 1 light blue Sixlet

MODIFICATIONS:
- **Super Princess Peach (alcoholic):** Add 1.5 ounces of cake-flavored vodka and 0.5 ounce of peach schnapps to the blender in step 1.

DIRECTIONS:
1. In a blender, combine the milk, ice cream, yogurt, peaches, vanilla cake mix, grenadine, ice (to taste), and food coloring (if using).
2. Blend until smooth and bright pink in color.
3. Transfer to the serving glass.
4. Garnish with whipped cream and gold sprinkles. Top with the lemon peel crowns.

34

RAINBOW ROAD

>>>>>>>>>>>>>>>>>>>

SERVING VESSEL: Hurricane, zombie, or another highball
SERVES: 1

Every *Mario Kart* game features an ascension to Rainbow Road, a glittering realm of wonder where the streets are paved with magical hues. The airy aura of Rainbow Road belies the course's savagery. Think Lisa Frank meets Mad Max. You want to survive to see the finish line? You want to stay on the road instead of getting red-shelled off the naked edge and into oblivion? Drive hard, friend.

No, not everyone is cut out to race across the Mario Kart universe's final plane of being, where the victor claims everything and the fallen losers get their atoms scattered until Lakitu gets around to reassembling them. There's lots of room on the sidelines if you just want to watch and sip on a fruity drink that hits your happy place with the impact of a blue shell.

FOR THE DRINK:

» 0.75 ounce Grenadine (page 8)
» 3 to 4 ounces orange-pineapple juice
» 2 to 3 ounces lemon-lime soda
» 0.5 ounce Blue Syrup (page 9)
» 0.75 ounce water
» 1 or 2 drops coconut extract (optional)

FOR THE GARNISH:

» 1 dollop whipped cream
» 1 sour rainbow belt candy

MODIFICATIONS:

» **A Sharp Turn (alcoholic):** Omit the coconut extract and mix 0.5 ounce of coconut rum into the orange-pineapple juice. Replace the blue syrup with blue curaçao liqueur and use 1.5 ounces of white rum instead of water.

DIRECTIONS:

1. Pour the grenadine into the bottom of the serving glass.
2. Add ice to fill the glass.
3. Slowly pour in the orange-pineapple juice until the glass is two-thirds full.
4. Slowly pour in the lemon-lime soda to fill.
5. In a separate small glass, mix the blue curaçao syrup, water, and coconut extract (if using). Slowly pour the blue curaçao mixture over the drink (the soda layer should turn blue).
6. Give the drink one or two quick stirs with a straw to blend the layers a bit.
7. Garnish with a whipped cream of your choice and a sour rainbow belt.

SERVING VESSEL:
Margarita or fishbowl
SERVES: 1

THE SPEEDY BLUE HEDGEHOG

Gotta drink fast! Gotta drink fast! Gotta drink faster, faster, faster, faster, faster! If you're a disciple of Sonic, the cerulean hedgehog who practically served as the mascot animal for the radical '90s, then you know nothing matters more in life than the thrill of chugging all your liquids until you sputter and choke. Sonic doesn't just run fast, no siree. He drinks fast. He eats fast. Sonic gets a pass because who's quick enough to slap him with a ticket?

You aren't a speedy blue hedgehog, so please run responsibly, eat slowly, and drink your delectable pineapple-coconut-flavored Speedy Blue Hedgehog with relish. (Not literal chopped pickles—that's nasty.)

FOR THE DRINK:
- 0.75 ounce Blue Syrup (page 9)
- 3 ounces coconut water (clear, not pink)
- 1.5 ounces pineapple juice
- 1 or 2 drops coconut extract
- 0.25 ounce lime juice

FOR THE GARNISH:
- Lime juice, for the rim
- Coarse sanding sugar, for the rim
- 2 maraschino cherries
- 3 or 4 pineapple rings

MODIFICATIONS:
- **Chaos (alcoholic):** Stir in 1.5 ounces of white rum, replace the blue syrup with blue curaçao liqueur, and swap the coconut extract for 0.5 ounces of coconut rum.

DIRECTIONS:
1. Rim the glass with lime juice and sanding sugar (page 14).
2. In a cocktail shaker filled with ice, add the blue curaçao syrup, coconut water, pineapple juice, coconut extract, and lime juice.
3. Shake for 10 to 15 seconds until well chilled.
4. Strain into the serving glass.
5. Garnish with cherries and pineapple rings.

SUPER MAR . . . GARITA

>>>>>>>>>>>>>>>>

SERVING VESSEL: Margarita, schooner or poco grande
SERVES: 1 to 2

When Mario debuted as a Nintendo character in 1981's arcade smash *Donkey Kong* (under his maiden name "Jumpman"), he was a blue-collar construction worker. Or a professional ape-harasser. Hey, sometimes you gotta wear a lot of hats on the job. But as Mario slipped down Brooklyn's pipes for more adventures in the Mushroom Kingdom, there was some debate over the iconic mascot's true origins. Is Mario (and by extension, Luigi) a citizen of New York City, or was he born and subsequently kidnapped in the Mushroom Kingdom?

The real answer? It doesn't matter. The only important thing is that Mario is willing to raise a glass with you as a friend. Can you pronounce *margarita*? Cool job, you're in Mario's good books. Let's-a drink and get into-a fistfight over the-a best pizza place in Brooklyn! *Woo-hoooo!*

FOR THE DRINK:
- 1 cup frozen strawberries
- 1 tablespoon white balsamic vinegar or 1 teaspoon regular balsamic
- 1 tablespoon Grenadine (page 8)
- ⅓ cup frozen limeade
- ¼ cup orange juice

FOR THE GARNISH:
- Lime juice or corn syrup, for the rim
- Coarse salt or sugar, for the rim
- 1 radish, cut into a mushroom shape

MODIFICATIONS:
- **Fire Mario:** Add half a Fresno chile or other hot chile pepper.
- **Let's A-go! (alcoholic):** Add 3 ounces of tequila and swap the orange juice for 2 ounces of aperol or an orange liqueur.

DIRECTIONS:
1. Rim the glass with the lime juice and salt.
2. In a blender, blend the strawberries, vinegar, grenadine, limeade, and orange for 1 to 2 minutes until smooth.
3. Pour into the serving glass.
4. Garnish with the "mushroom" radish.

SERVING VESSEL: Rocks or lowball
SERVES: 1

WARIOPEAR: SHAKE IT!

<<<<<<<<<<<<<<<<

It's a weird topic to even think about, but Wario is one of the most underhanded characters in Nintendo's marketable menagerie—and that's because he *isn't* marketed, certainly not to the point of Mario, Luigi, or Link. Nintendo lets Wario roam to free-feed, like a cow or, more suitably, a pig. And while Nintendo looks the other way, Wario exercises unregulated capitalism on any sucker in his vicinity. Of particular note is how he literally shakes his foes down to relieve them of their lunch money. Some little dude's out there living their life, and Wario just grabs them and shakes them like a piggy bank for every last coin they own.

Horrible method, but effective. Wario's got cash, Wario's got property, and more than that, he's got buddies who help him in his money-making schemes. They're not loser friends, either. Heck, Wario's friends are cooler than yours, guaranteed, and they all have his (gaseous) back. How does he do it? Maybe it's the drinks he makes. They're supposed to be great. It takes a prickly pear to serve up a prickly pear as a refreshment.

FOR THE DRINK:
- 1 ounce prickly pear syrup
- 0.25 ounce Blue Syrup (page 9)
- 0.5 ounce lemon juice
- 3 ounces white cranberry juice
- 1 or 2 drops Saline (page 9)

FOR THE GARNISH:
- Lemon peel cut into a W shape

MODIFICATIONS:
- **WarioPear: Spiked! (alcoholic):** Add 1.5 ounces of vodka and swap the blue syrup for 0.25 ounce of blue curaçao liqueur.

DIRECTIONS:
1. In a cocktail shaker filled with ice, add the prickly pear syrup, blue curaçao syrup, lemon juice, cranberry juice, and saline.
2. Shake for 10 to 15 seconds until well chilled.
3. Strain into the serving glass.
4. Garnish with the lemon peel.

MULTIPLAYER MOCKTAILS

47	Cooldown Cooler
48	DK's Stolen Banana Horde
51	The Imposter (Kinda Sus)
52	The Loot Llama
55	Magicant Mojo
56	The Nook Store Special
59	Tarrey Town Wedding

COOLDOWN COOLER

>>>>>>>>>>>>>>>>

SERVING VESSEL:
1-gallon pitcher
or drink dispenser
SERVES: 6 to 8

"Cooldown" is a misnomer in the context of gaming. Nobody chills while waiting for their grayed-out skill icon to chug back to life. They swear, they howl, and then they die because the vital spell they tried to cast was a nanosecond too late. Then the DPS usually blames the Healer, who blames the Tank, who wasn't able to stop the DPS from jumping into AOEs like the ocean on a hot day.

Disappointment on the battlefield turns into resentment, which turns into fandom drama, which turns into a tire fire that will burn until your grandchildren are dead. If you're the leader of a Guild or a Free Company, make sure your party members drink something cold, smooth, and calming before heading into the fray. Breathe. Chill. So what if the Healer can't manage her MP for beans? So what if the DPS has the brains and grace of the Tasmanian Devil? So what if the Tank is picking his butt instead of turning on his stance *yet again*? We're all gonna die anyway.

FOR THE DRINK:
- 1 cucumber, sliced
- 2 limes, sliced
- 2 star fruit and/or peeled kiwis, sliced (optional)
- 4 cups brewed jasmine green tea, chilled
- 4 cups coconut water, chilled
- 1 can frozen limeade

FOR THE GARNISH:
- Fresh mint sprigs
- Lime wedges or wheels
- Sliced cucumber

DIRECTIONS:
1. In the pitcher or drink dispenser, combine the cucumber, limes, and star fruit.
2. Add the green tea and coconut water and stir.
3. Stir in the frozen limeade until dissolved.
4. Add ice to taste.

SERVING VESSEL: Large punch bowl or 1-gallon pitcher
SERVES: 8 to 10

DK'S STOLEN BANANA HORDE

<<<<<<<<<<<<<<<<<

Did you know that, after you beat *Donkey Kong Country* for the SNES and save your game, you can enter Donkey Kong's formerly depleted banana hoard and find it restored in its golden glory? That begs the question why Donkey Kong feels the need to run through the jungle all over again. Does he just want to give King K. Rool a painful reminder that there's only one banana-scarfer in town, and it's him? (And maybe Diddy Kong?)

In any case, take note of how Donkey Kong's recovered hoard is pristine. Not a single bruised banana. If you're a fan of the tropical fruit, you know how they turn brown and mushy if you so much as glance at them. Whatever else you might say about the Kremlings, they're obviously some damn fine fruit-keepers. You, however, are not an anthropomorphic alligator with a green (scaled) thumb, so just take those hopeless bananas of yours and mash them down into a drink before the fruit flies carry them and your children away.

FOR THE DRINK:
» 5 ripe bananas
» ⅓ cup light brown sugar
» 3 cups water
» 12 ounces frozen limeade concentrate
» 4 cups orange-pineapple juice
» 24 to 32 ounces ginger ale

FOR THE GARNISH:
» Banana slices

MODIFICATIONS:
» **Funky's Flights (alcoholic):** Add 1 cup of dark and/or spiced rum and ½ cup of banana liqueur.

DIRECTIONS:
1. In a blender, blend the bananas, light brown sugar, and water until smooth.
2. Transfer to the serving vessel. Mix in the limeade concentrate.
3. Add a cup or two of ice, if desired.
4. Add the orange-pineapple juice, then top off with ginger ale to taste.
5. Garnish with the banana slices.

THE IMPOSTER (KINDA SUS)

>>>>>>>>>>>>>>>>>

SERVING VESSEL: Large punch bowl or 1-gallon pitcher
SERVES: 8 to 10

If you're trapped in the middle of space on a ship that's harboring a well-disguised life-form that thirsts for blood, you probably shouldn't drink anything that's handed to you. But it'll look suspicious if you *don't* drink because what are you, some kinda alien impostor that lacks human mouthparts? *Hmmmm?*

So, you drink. Instant betrayal! The drink is alcoholic, and you're only fifteen. The space cops are going to kick your criminal ass out the airlock, impostor or not, and your mom is gonna be so mad.

Surprise! There's no booze in the drink—just a suggestion of rum. Now hold still while the imposter sticks his proboscis in your belly, drinks your cocktail secondhand, and shoves your shriveled husk behind some boxes.

· ·

FOR THE DRINK:

- 3 cups fruit punch, chilled
- 1½ cups pineapple juice, chilled
- 1½ cups passion fruit juice, chilled
- ½ cup lime juice
- ½ cup Grenadine (page 8)
- 1 to 2 teaspoons rum extract
- ¼ cup apple cider vinegar
- 1 to 2 teaspoons aromatic bitters (optional)
- 24 to 32 ounces ginger ale, chilled

FOR THE GARNISH:

- 8 to 10 maraschino cherries or frozen raspberries
- 1 orange, sliced
- 1 lime, sliced
- 1 lemon, sliced
- Other color fruit pieces

MODIFICATIONS:

- **Sabotage:** Use 1½ cups of real rum instead of the rum extract. Add ½ cup of hibiscus, tropical, or orange liqueur in place of the apple cider vinegar.

DIRECTIONS:

1. In a serving vessel, stir the punch, pineapple juice, passion fruit juice, lime juice, and grenadine until well combined.
2. Stir in the rum extract, apple cider vinegar, and bitters to taste. Start with a small amount, then taste and adjust until it's to your liking. These three should give the drink a suspiciously alcohol-like kick.
3. Add 2 cups of standard ice, or to taste.
4. Top with ginger ale to taste.
5. Garnish with cherries, citrus wheels, and various colorful fruits to represent your favorite *Among Us* colors.

SERVING VESSEL: Punch bowl
SERVES: 6 to 8

THE LOOT LLAMA

<<<<<<<<<<<<<<<<<

Epic's epic battle royale game *Fortnite* is a divider between millennials and Gen Z. That doesn't mean older folks should avoid playing *Fortnite*. Gen Z kids are pretty smart. They can smell age creeping on us, which appeals to their softer side. A Gen Z player might even protect a less experienced millennial player—at least until the storm closes in and Peter Griffin, Goku, and Spider-Man are forced to turn their warm-muzzled guns at each other, bodies piled around them, tears brimming in their eyes.

If you want to reward the *Fortnite* players in your family who hold off on shooting their elders until the last possible minute, this Loot Llama is guaranteed to please. It's sweet, fizzy, creamy, and filled with little gummy delights waiting to be "busted out" of their ice cube containments. It's tasty enough to make you do whatever dance is popular with the kids now.

FOR THE DRINK:

» ½ cup Blue Syrup (page 9)
» ½ cup cream of coconut (the syrup, such as Coco Reàl or Coco Lopez)
» 12 ounces frozen limeade concentrate
» 12 to 24 ounces water, chilled
» 24 to 32 ounces lemon-lime soda, chilled
» 8 to 10 large scoops ube ice cream (or another purple ice cream)

FOR THE LOOT:

» Various colorful candies and/or fruits (such as gummies, sour candies, kiwis, etc.)
» 2 to 4 ice cube trays

DIRECTIONS:

1. To make the loot, place the various fruits and candies into the ice cube trays, then fill them with water and freeze until solid.
2. In a punch bowl, mix the blue curaçao syrup, cream of coconut, and limeade concentrate until well combined.
3. Stir in the water.
4. Add the ice cubes from the molds. You can add more ice, if desired.
5. Top with the lemon-lime soda.
6. Add the scoops of ube ice cream on top.

MAGICANT MOJO

>>>>>>>>>>>>>>>>>>

SERVING VESSEL: Punch bowl
SERVES: 8 to 12

Magicant is a magical land of thoughts and dreams that exists in Shigesato Itoi's celebrated *Mother/EarthBound* RPG series. Magicant's pastel colors, deep purple sea, and pink trees, which look similar to the fuzzy saplings Dr. Seuss's Lorax once spoke for, give the land an unreal but uneasy aura—a place where dreams lie comfortably astride nightmares.

But something about Magicant encourages you to challenge those nightmares and overcome your weaknesses. Mother's hero, Ninten, and his maybe-grandson, Ness from *EarthBound*, both visit Magicant to test their limits and break them. But it turns out surviving in Magicant is simple; it's the void beyond that'll swallow you whole. Make the party a colorful, fruity drink to cling to when you're inevitably made to forget that anything resembling love, warmth, and friendship exists beyond the voracious black hole created by the mind-warping grief of a lonely alien baby.

FOR THE DRINK:

- 2 cups concord grape juice or other grape drink, chilled (try to get one with a bright purple color)
- 3 cups pineapple juice, chilled
- 2 tablespoons Blue Syrup (page 9)
- ½ teaspoon edible luster dust (optional)
- 24 ounces blackberry ginger ale, chilled
- 10 large scoops rainbow sherbet

DIRECTIONS:

1. In a punch bowl, combine the grape juice, pineapple juice, blue curaçao syrup, and luster dust (if using).
2. Add about 2 cups of ice, if desired.
3. Top with the chilled blackberry ginger ale.
4. Top with the rainbow sherbet.

MODIFICATIONS:

- **Magicant Bat:** Add 1½ cups of vodka and ½ cup of raspberry liqueur along with the juices in step 1.

SERVING VESSEL:
1-gallon pitcher
or drink dispenser
SERVES: 10 to 12

THE NOOK STORE SPECIAL

<<<<<<<<<<<<<<<<

Tom Nook, the ring-tailed merchant who rules over your property and soul in the *Animal Crossing* series, knows there's good money in scamming young people. New arrivals to *Animal Crossing* are soft and homesick—easy to break down and rope into indentured servitude, yes yes.

The wily tanuki invariably puts you to work as soon as you step off the train, the bus, or whatever chariot delivers you to your new home. Listen, just put on the uniform, stock the shelves, and say "Yes yes" as required. There's a house in it for you, and by Tortimer's ghost, deals like that don't come around twice in a lifetime.

If Nook likes you, he might let you try some of the blue fruity concoction sitting on the counter. Don't expect anything alcoholic; booze is pricey. Do you think bells grow on trees? What do you mean "they do"? Get outta here.

FOR THE DRINK:
- 1 orange, sliced
- 1 lemon, sliced
- 1 apple, sliced
- 1 peach, sliced
- 6 cups white grape juice*
- 4 cups white cranberry-peach juice*
- ⅓ cup Blue Syrup (page 9)
- 1 liter lemon-lime soda, chilled

FOR THE GARNISH:
- 1 to 2 cups fruit pieces (use a colorful variety)

MODIFICATIONS:
- **Vacation Juice (alcoholic):** Replace the white grape juice with 2 bottles of moscato and the blue syrup with blue curaçao. Add ¾ cup of peach schnapps.

*Select juices that are very light in color, with no additional coloring added.

DIRECTIONS:
1. In a pitcher or drink dispenser, combine the orange, lemon, apple, peach, grape juice, and cranberry-peach juice and let sit in the refrigerator for at least 4 hours, up to overnight.
2. Remove from the refrigerator. Add the blue curaçao syrup until the mixture turns a nice bright blue color.
3. If desired, use fruit cutters on a variety of colorful fruits to use as garnish and add them to the pitcher.
4. Add ice and top off with the lemon-lime soda to taste.

TARREY TOWN WEDDING

>>>>>>>>>>>>>>>>

SERVING VESSEL:
1 or 2 watermelon halves or a punch bowl
SERVES: 6 to 8

Legend of Zelda: Breath of the Wild isn't simply a game about beating up Ganon and saving Zelda. It's also a story of renewed hopes in a fledgling civilization that's just starting to get back on its feet after the Calamity. Link fights to shelter that hope as much as he fights to shelter Hyrule.

Tarrey Town, the little village Link helps construct, is at the heart of the Hyrulians' will to carry on. It's where different members of Hyrule's races gather to build homes and set up shop. The finished village is crowned with a wedding between a Gerudo woman and a Hylian man with a sick 'stache. Neither of them have any idea if things will work out between them, but there's nothing like a sweet, fruity drink to set new couples at ease.

FOR THE DRINK:
» 1 medium seedless watermelon
» 1 cup guava nectar, chilled
» ⅓ cup sweetened condensed milk
» 3 cups whole milk or carton (not canned) coconut milk
» 24 ounces lemon-lime soda, chilled

FOR THE GARNISH:
» ½ honeydew melon
» 1 dragon fruit, halved

MODIFICATIONS:
» **A Toast to Love and Guidelines Compliance! (alcoholic):** Add one 375-mL bottle of classic or watermelon soju. Watermelon-flavored rum or watermelon-flavored vodka can be used instead.

DIRECTIONS:
1. Using a sharp knife, cut the watermelon in half. Remember to keep the watermelon half intact if you are planning to use it as a punch bowl.
2. Using a large melon baller or an ice-cream scoop, scoop out the flesh of the watermelon. If you want to cut the watermelon pieces into hearts, use a knife to remove pieces of watermelon, slicing them about ½ inch thick. Use a fruit cutter or cookie cutter to make hearts. You will want about a cup of watermelon pieces and about a cup of watermelon juice. (A nice, juicy watermelon will produce about this much just from being cut up. You can reserve any extra watermelon flesh for another purpose.)
3. Use a melon baller to scoop balls from the inside of the honeydew melon and the dragon fruit.
4. Set the fruit aside in the fridge, along with the watermelon halves, if using. If the watermelon halves are not sitting level, use a sharp knife to cut the bottoms flat. In a mixing bowl, stir the guava nectar and sweetened condensed milk until the condensed milk dissolves. Add the whole milk and stir until well combined.
5. Remove the watermelon halves from the fridge. Add ice to them, if desired. Add the lemon-lime soda and let it fizz out, then stir in the milk mixture.
6. Serve the punch inside the watermelon halves or in a large punch bowl. Garnish with the watermelon hearts and dragon fruit and melon balls.

63 Amy Rose's Piko Piko Hammer

64 Caulk the Wagon and Float It

67 Cherry-Eating Ghostbuster

68 Do a Barrel Roll!

71 FINISH HIM

72 Gold Chocobo

75 Half the World

76 Metroidvania

79 Moscow M.U.L.E.

80 The Power of the Dragon

83 The Secret of Monkey Island

84 SHORYUKEN

87 The Spread Gun

88 Yellow Yorgle's Yorsh

AMY ROSE'S PIKO PIKO HAMMER

SERVING VESSEL: Highball
SERVES: 1

Amy Rose is a headstrong strawberry-pink hedgehog who knows how to swing a hammer like Dani California. The Piko Piko hammer looks like a toy, but any badnik who's ever had their jaw hinge separated from their metal cranium with a single blow would tell you otherwise if they could.

Amy Rose has graduated from a one-note fangirl who literally clings to Sonic to an avid protector of her friends. She shoulders her team's worries and dreams, which is a heavy burden to bear. So, once in a while, Amy Rose settles back on a hammock and slides into Girl Drink Drunk Zone. She's entitled to it.

FOR THE DRINK:

- 1 to 3 strawberries, sliced
- 0.25 ounce lemon juice
- 2 ounces navy-strength gin
- ¼ teaspoon rose water (optional)
- 0.75 ounce strawberry or raspberry liqueur
- 0.5 ounce orgeat
- 2 to 3 ounces sparkling rosé

FOR THE GARNISH:

- 2 or 3 strawberry slices
- Lemon peel
- Toothpick
- Cocktail skewer

MODIFICATIONS:

- **The Love Hammer (nonalcoholic):** Omit the gin or use a gin substitute (page 16). Substitute strawberry syrup or Grenadine (page 8) for the strawberry liqueur. Replace the rosé with sparkling apple-cranberry juice or another sweet, pink, and fruity sparkling beverage.

DIRECTIONS:

1. To make the garnish, use a toothpick to skewer two or three strawberry slices through the center. Use scissors or a sharp knife to cut two circles around the same size of the strawberry slices from the lemon peel. Skewer the lemon peel circles on either end of the skewered strawberry slices to create Amy's hammer. Skewer this through the center with a cocktail skewer.
2. In a serving glass, gently muddle the strawberries and lemon juice.
3. Add the gin, rose water (if using), liqueur, and orgeat.
4. Add ice to taste.
5. Top with sparkling rosé.
6. Garnish with the "hammer" you made in step 1.

SERVING VESSEL:
Glass mug or
can-shaped glass
SERVES: 1

CAULK THE WAGON AND FLOAT IT

Traveling the titular *Oregon Trail* on the Apple II was a rite of passage for '80s kids, one that we handily flubbed again and again. The innumerable tombstones that litter the dirt road tell the history of POOPFACE, the fearless but unlucky party leader, and dear companions like JESUS and MARIO and SKELETOR, who all died of turbo dysentery or something.

Death by drowning was especially popular. One of the first big decisions you must make after you hit the road is whether or not to pay a ferryman or a Native American guide for safe passage across the Kansas River. Your other option is to save a few pennies by caulking the wagon and floating it, which is a great way to lose everything you own ten minutes after starting the game. Hopefully the rich, dark flavor of an alcoholic root beer float will take your mind off your dead firstborn. He belongs to the river now.

FOR THE DRINK:
» 2 or 3 scoops coffee ice cream
» 1.5 ounces whiskey or bourbon
» 0.75 ounce coffee liqueur
» 3 or 4 drops sassafras or root beer bitters (optional)
» 4 to 6 ounces stout or dark beer, chilled

MODIFICATIONS:
» **The Broken Wagon Wheel (nonalcoholic):** Omit the whiskey or use a whiskey substitute. Substitute a shot of espresso or cold brew concentrate for the coffee liqueur, or omit it for less or zero caffeine. Replace the stout with sarsaparilla soda or a high-quality "old-fashioned" root beer.
» **The Snakebite:** Replace the coffee liqueur with ginger liqueur. Swap ginger beer for the stout. Instead of coffee ice cream, use vanilla. Swap spicy bitters instead of sarsaparilla.
» **Found Wild Fruit:** Use marionberry or blackberry ice cream and swap the coffee liqueur with marionberry liqueur or blackberry brandy. Instead of stout, use a fruited beer or berry-flavored malt beverage. Garnish with fresh berries or berry syrup.

DIRECTIONS:
1. Put the ice cream in the mug.
2. Add the whiskey, coffee liqueur, and bitters (if using) to the glass.
3. Top with stout to fill.

CHERRY-EATING GHOSTBUSTER

>>>>>>>>>>>>>>>>>>>>

SERVING VESSEL: Martini or cocktail
SERVES: 1

We're not talking about the Ghostbusters who piss off glam gods and look into ghost traps after being told not to. We're talking about the granddaddy of ghostbusters, the creature that burns sunlight-yellow in the sullen blue corridors of the mazes he's doomed to run forever. We're talking about PAC-MAN, the great GHOST-scarfer who lives only to fill his borderless belly with the plasma of his enemies.

It's hard to be PAC-MAN. The second he makes a mistake, the GHOSTS gobble him up. Then *he* becomes . . . chunks of whatever he's made of. Yeah, he just floats in the GHOSTS' tummies until he reforms at the starting line. But there are pleasures that soothe PAC-MAN's pain when the hunter becomes the hunted. CHERRIES, for example. When they appear, he can eat 'em up and feel good about himself. If PAC-MAN has time, maybe he can fix a CHERRY drink. Mix one up for your papa and don't skimp on the vodka.

FOR THE DRINK:
» 1.5 ounces vodka
» 0.75 ounce maraschino liqueur
» 0.75 ounce Licor 43 or other yellow vanilla liqueur
» 0.5 ounce lemon juice
» 3 or 4 dashes cherry bitters (optional)

FOR THE GARNISH:
» 2 maraschino cherries (with stems)
» Lemon peel
» Cocktail skewer

DIRECTIONS:
1. To make the garnish, cut the lemon peel into a Pac-Man shape and skewer it along with two stemmed maraschino cherries.
2. In a cocktail shaker filled with ice, add the vodka, maraschino liqueur, Licor 43, lemon juice, and bitters (if using).
3. Shake for 10 to 15 seconds until well chilled.
4. Strain into the serving glass.
5. Garnish with the Pac-Man skewer.

SERVING VESSEL: Rocks
SERVES: 1

DO A BARREL ROLL!

<<<<<<<<<<<<<<<<

A little-known secret about the Star Fox team is that they're a menagerie of crack-shot space pilots, but they once mixed up the instruction to "Do a barrel roll" with "Roll out the barrel." The barrel was indeed rolled out, and by the time the whole thing passed, Slippy was forced to sheepishly call his dad for money to spring the *Great Fox* from Lylat's galactic impound lot.

The team now tries to be more careful about how they celebrate their victories over the vicious ape-man Andross. Fox, Peppy, and Falco all have Post-It notes on their glove compartments of their *Arwings* reminding them to be responsible. Unfortunately, that restraint goes out the window as soon as the latest bounty check from General Pepper clears. Then they hit up Corneria, Fox orders that one cute drink that's garnished with orange peel fox ears, everyone loses their minds, and the *Great Fox* is behind bars again.

FOR THE DRINK:
- 1.5 ounces barrel-proof bourbon
- 2 ounces carrot juice or carrot-ginger juice
- 0.75 ounce amaretto
- 0.25 ounce pure maple syrup (ideally barrel aged)
- 3 or 4 dashes walnut and/or pecan bitters

FOR THE GARNISH:
- Maple syrup, for the rim (optional)
- Cinnamon sugar, for the rim (optional)
- 2 orange slices

MODIFICATIONS:
- **The Aileron Roll (nonalcoholic):** Omit the bourbon or use a bourbon substitute. Use barrel-aged pure maple syrup and increase the amount to 0.75 ounce. Replace the amaretto with amaretto syrup or orgeat.

DIRECTIONS:
1. Rim the glass with maple syrup and cinnamon sugar, if desired.
2. In a cocktail shaker filled with ice, add the bourbon, carrot juice, amaretto, maple syrup, and walnut bitters.
3. Shake for 10 to 15 seconds.
4. Strain into the serving glass.
5. Garnish with two orange slices on either side of the glass (so they look like bunny ears).

FINISH HIM

>>>>>>>>>>>>>>>>>>

SERVING VESSEL:
1-pint glass and
2 shot glasses
SERVES: 1

In the *Mortal Kombat* series, when you hear the announcer growl, "Finish him," you know you're a half second away from watching one fighter pound the other fighter into a quivering jelly of blood and viscera. It's as much part of video games' classic voice clips as "Run, coward!" and "It's-a me, Mario!"

In the '90s, however, "Finish him" became the two most loaded words ever uttered in a video game until that point. Concerned parents rallied over the first *Mortal Kombat*'s outrageous violence, even though there wasn't a kid over the age of two who was shocked at the sight of Kano ripping a ridiculously enlarged heart out of Scorpion's chest.

Nevertheless, the Entertainment Software Ratings Board was born to throw a sop to these outraged parents. It's a silly moment to look back on, but it's whimsical to look back at the issues we thought were important in the '90s. Oh, to afford such naivety again.

FOR THE DRINK:

- 1 ounce white rum
- 5 ounces energy drink, chilled
- 0.5 ounce Grenadine (page 8)
- 2 ounces strawberry or pomegranate liqueur
- 2 or 3 dashes aromatic bitters
- 1 or 2 drops Saline (page 9)

DIRECTIONS:

1. Pour the rum and energy drink into a standard pint glass so it's a little less than half full.
2. In a cocktail shaker filled with ice, add the grenadine, strawberry liqueur, bitters, and saline.
3. Shake for 10 to 15 seconds until well chilled.
4. Strain into two shot glasses.
5. Set the two shots on top of the drink so they hold each other in place.
6. To perform the fatality, take one shot and down it, letting the other fall into the energy drink and rum. Then, drink the energy drink and rum with the shot in it.

SERVING VESSEL:
Sour or coupe
SERVES: 1

GOLD CHOCOBO

<<<<<<<<<<<<<<<<

The *Final Fantasy* series' chocobos are ostrich-size birds of burden that are prized for their swiftness. Standard chocobos bear bright yellow plumage, but they've also been bred excessively to display vivid shades of red, blue, and green. Very selective breeding can even produce a chocobo with jet-black plumage that pairs well with sad music.

If you breed chocobos both **excessively** and **selectively** and cross bloodlines that **shouldn't** be crossed, there's a slight chance you'll hatch a chocobo with splendorous golden plumage. Do not be confused. This chocobo is actually a messenger god that's come to drag your soul to Big Bird Hell for your crimes against nature. Treat yourself to a last drink and take the memory of that gold feather dissolving against your tongue down to the Infernal Pit of Kweh.

FOR THE DRINK:
» 1.5 ounces gin
» 1 ounce yellow chartreuse or Licor 43
» 0.75 ounce lemon juice
» 0.5 ounce elderflower liqueur
» 1 egg white or 3 tablespoons aquafaba, for foam (optional)
» ¼ teaspoon edible gold luster dust (optional)
» 2 or 3 drops Saline (page 9) or pinch kosher salt

FOR THE GARNISH:
» Lemon peel
» Gold sprinkles or gold leaf (optional)

DIRECTIONS:
1. Use kitchen shears or a sharp knife to cut the lemon peel into a feather shape. If you'd like, paint the lemon peel with gold luster dust and skewer with a cocktail skewer. Set this aside.
2. In a cocktail shaker, combine the gin, yellow chartreuse, lemon juice, elderflower liqueur, egg white or aquafaba (if using), gold luster dust (if using), and saline.
3. Shake for 25 to 30 seconds until foamy.
4. Add ice to the cocktail shaker.
5. Shake for another 10 to 15 seconds until well chilled.
6. Strain into the serving glass. Let it settle for 15 to 20 seconds.
7. Garnish with gold sprinkles or gold leaf, if using, and the lemon peel.

HALF THE WORLD

>>>>>>>>>>>>>>>>>>

SERVING VESSEL:
Rocks
SERVES: 1

In the shadowed realm of Alefgard, there exists a legend that a warrior, a direct descendant of the great hero Erdrick, will appear from heaven. This savior will take up Erdrick's arms and slay the Dragon Lord, whose dark magic keeps Alefgard bound.

Dragons are wily creatures, and they well know the greed that lies in the pits of every man's heart. It is the same greed that nestles in their own bosom, coin for coin, jewel for jewel. A wise dragon knows when to negotiate, even if it means giving up half their hoard to a fallen, frustrated "hero." Better wounded pride than a wounded body.

But dragons also understand that some deals only need to last as long as the glasses are raised, the rye is quaffed, and the poison starts to rot the body. Thank Rubiss, no Scion of Erdrick would be fool enough to take up a wyrm's offer.

FOR THE DRINK:

» 1 ounce rye whiskey
» 0.75 ounce red bittersweet aperitif (such as Campari)
» 0.5 ounce sweet (red) vermouth
» 0.5 ounce ancho chile liqueur or red cinnamon schnapps
» 3 or 4 dashes aromatic bitters

FOR THE GARNISH:

» 1 Luxardo cherry or other black cocktail cherry

DIRECTIONS:

1. In a cocktail shaker filled with ice, add the whiskey, aperitif, vermouth, ancho chile liqueur, and bitters.
2. Shake for 10 to 15 seconds until well chilled.
3. Strain into a serving glass.
4. Garnish with a Luxardo cherry.

SERVING VESSEL:
Tall shot glass
SERVES: 1

METROIDVANIA

<<<<<<<<<<<<<<<<

When electronic junk mail—i.e., "spam"—began to proliferate, the actual meat magicians behind the Spam food product suggested that society adopt an alternative name for the deluge advertising "pen one five" pills. Ten thousand years later, "spam" endures as a descriptor as well as a problem.

Similarly, critics of the "Metroidvania" action-game sub-genre name recommend another, more descriptive moniker. "Search-Action"? Nah. Metroidvania is the best game genre descriptor of all time. If that makes you mad, you'd better drink about it.

FOR THE DRINK:

» 0.5 ounce peach schnapps
» 0.5 ounce maraschino liqueur
» 0.25 ounce white chocolate cream liqueur or other cream liqueur
» 4 or 5 drops Grenadine (page 8)
» 4 or 5 drops sour apple schnapps or melon liqueur

DIRECTIONS:

1. Pour the peach schnapps and maraschino liqueur into the shot glass.
2. Hold a spoon on the surface of the drink and slowly pour the white chocolate cream liqueur so it overflows and floats on top of the drink.
3. Add the grenadine until it becomes too heavy and falls to the bottom. It will take some of the cream layer with it and create spires on the bottom.
4. Add drops of sour apple schnapps or melon liqueur until it settles under the cream layer.

MOSCOW M.U.L.E.

>>>>>>>>>>>>>>>>>>>

SERVING VESSEL:
Copper mug
SERVES: 1

On the faraway planet of Irata, settlers scramble for territory and inventory. The economics of supply and demand drive everything that happens in this new world, and competition is fierce. Can you even count on a single friend? Someone who'll share a drink with you and not try to screw with your numbers? Maybe just one: Your faithful Multiple Use Labor Elements robot. Your M.U.L.E. Whatever needs doing, the ol' chrome boy is always up for it. You might say he's a real jackass, but we mean it in the nicest possible way.

FOR THE DRINK:
» 1.5 ounces vodka
» 0.5 ounce lime juice
» 1 to 2 ounces peach or pear nectar
» 2 or 3 dashes orange bitters
» 3 to 4 ounces ginger beer

FOR THE GARNISH:
» Candied ginger or rock candy
» Lime wheels or slices

DIRECTIONS:
1. Fill a copper mug two-thirds full with ice.
2. Add the vodka, lime juice, peach nectar, and bitters.
3. Give the drink a quick stir.
4. Top with ginger beer to fill.
5. Garnish with candied ginger and lime wheels.

SERVING VESSEL:
2 shot glasses
SERVES: 1

THE POWER OF THE DRAGON

The *Double Dragon* twins Billy and Jimmy Lee are the wayward sons of the belt-scrolling beat-'em-up genre. Armed with their fists, pipes, knives, and whips, the boys cleaned up the pestilent streets of postapocalyptic New York City when their girlfriend, Marian, was kidnapped by the evil Shadow Boss. There's nary a Nintendo owner alive who didn't have a copy of *Double Dragon* or its sequel—in which the Lee brothers get revenge on the Shadow Boss's goons for bodying Marian. Daaang.

Our boys went hard until a shift in *Double Dragon*'s ownership turned them into cartoon action heroes who wussed out on using contact violence against bad guys because it was the '90s and we thought we had real problems. At least the cartoon show's theme song is worth raising a couple of glasses to.

FOR THE BILLY:

» 0.5 ounce clear mint schnapps
» 0.5 ounce Blue Syrup (page 8)
» 0.25 ounce lime juice

FOR THE JIMMY:

» 0.5 ounce hot cinnamon schnapps
» 0.5 ounce amaretto
» 0.25 ounce Grenadine (page 8)

DIRECTIONS:

1. To make the Billy, in a cocktail shaker filled with ice, add the clear mint schnapps, blue curaçao, and lime juice.
2. Shake for 10 to 15 seconds until well chilled.
3. Strain into a shot glass.
4. Dump the ice out of the cocktail shaker and rinse it out, then add fresh ice.
5. To make the Jimmy, in the cocktail shaker, combine the hot cinnamon schnapps, amaretto, and grenadine.
6. Shake for 10 to 15 seconds until well chilled.
7. Strain into a separate shot glass.
8. Drink one shot in one swig, then the other.

THE SECRET OF MONKEY ISLAND

SERVING VESSEL: Glass mug, goblet, or highball
SERVES: 1

>>>>>>>>>>>>>>>>>>>>

We would never dream of speaking for the great (?) pirate Guybrush Threepwood, but sometimes you have to speak a man's mind for him. Listen, our boy Threepwood is tired of drinking grog. **Dead** tired. Like, zombie pirate-level dead tired.

I bet he's not the only pirate who'd enjoy something different against his palette. Oh, I hear your mumbled "Ayes." Don't pretend otherwise. Here's what you need to do. Keep the rum—*always* keep the rum—but don't be chintzy with the sweet stuff! Bananas! Root beer! A little sour lime to keep things grounded. Just what you need to boost you up before a duel of sharp swords and sharper words.

FOR THE DRINK:
» 1.5 ounces spiced rum
» 0.5 ounce banana liqueur
» 0.25 ounce lime juice
» 3 ounces root beer

FOR THE GARNISH:
» 1 banana slice
» 2 cocktail swords

DIRECTIONS:
1. Optionally, using a knife or a skull-shaped fruit cutter, cut the banana slice into a skull shape.
2. In a tall glass, combine the rum, banana liqueur, and lime juice.
3. Give the drink a quick stir.
4. Fill the glass two-thirds full with ice.
5. Add root beer to fill.
6. Skewer the banana skull with two cocktail swords and use it to garnish the drink.

SERVING VESSEL:
Highball
SERVES: 1

SHORYUKEN

<<<<<<<<<<<<<<<<

Everyone knows the battle cry that accompanies Ken and Ryu's lethal uppercut in *Street Fighter*. When you need to obliterate someone's chin, screaming the Dragon Punch's true name as you leap will give you that flourish you crave deep down. The Shoryuken is *the* iconic fighting game move because it's amazing, not because most of us never got the hang of shouting "Tatsumaki." Heck, Ken just immolates his wrist and leaps for his enemies' throats. That's baaadass.

Sidenote: Are you an old person who played *Street Fighter II* when it initially hit the arcades and the SNES? Do the words *TIGER*, *TIGER*, *TIGER* still echo in your dreams? Slam a few strong drinks and try to forget how many quarters Sagat siphoned from your pockets with his cheap kickboxing schtick. (So many quarters.)

FOR THE DRINK:
» 2 ounces Japanese whiskey or scotch
» 0.75 ounce orange liqueur
» 3 ounces mango juice
» ½ yuzu or small lemon
» 4 or 5 drops spicy or aromatic bitters

FOR THE GARNISH:
» Lime juice, for the rim
» Shichimi togarashi, for the rim
» 1 or 2 bird's-eye chiles (optional)
» 1 squeezed yuzu or small lemon half
» 3 to 5 dashes spicy and/or aromatic bitters
» 0.25 ounce overproof rum (or any liquor or liqueur over 80 proof will do)

DIRECTIONS:
1. Rim the glass with lime juice and shichimi togarashi.
2. Fill the glass with crushed ice.
3. In a cocktail shaker filled with standard ice, add the whiskey, orange liqueur, mango juice, and the squeezed juice from the yuzu. Set the squeezed yuzu aside (you will use it later for the garnish).
4. Shake for 10 to 15 seconds until well chilled.
5. Strain into the serving glass.
6. Add 3 to 5 dashes of the bitters on top of the drink.
7. Place the squeezed yuzu on top of the drink and fill it with the overproof rum. Use a long-necked lighter to light it on fire. Garnish the drink with bird's-eye chiles, if desired. Once the fire burns out, you can squeeze any remaining liquid from the charred yuzu into the drink.

THE SPREAD GUN

>>>>>>>>>>>>>>>>>

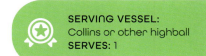

SERVING VESSEL: Collins or other highball
SERVES: 1

If you ever need to make yourself smile, just picture the *Contra* series' meat slab mascots, Bill and Lance, walking into the kind of bar that sells cocktails. Imagine them gawking at the gentle lighting, marveling over the sleek bar, and whispering in hoarse voices after the barmaid asks them what they'd like to drink.

"What is this place?" Bill mutters.

"Keep your eyes peeled," Lance returns.

Then imagine the duo somehow slipping into a booth and slamming back a tasty drink named after the most celebrated gun in their arsenal. Then they both hurl their glasses to the ground and start a fistfight . . . Too far?

FOR THE DRINK:
- 2 ounces vodka
- 0.75 ounce maraschino liqueur
- 0.25 ounce lemon juice
- 2 to 3 dashes cherry bitters (optional)
- 3 to 4 ounces lemon-lime soda
- 2 tablespoons strawberry popping boba or other red popping bobas

FOR THE GARNISH:
- 1 to 3 maraschino cherries

DIRECTIONS:
1. Fill the glass two-thirds full with ice.
2. Add the vodka, maraschino liqueur, lemon juice, and bitters (if using) to the serving glass.
3. Add lemon-lime soda to fill.
4. Add the popping boba and maraschino cherries, allowing them to fall to the bottom of the glass.
5. Drink with a boba straw.

SERVING VESSEL:
Pint glass, pilsner, or other beer glass
SERVES: 1

YELLOW YORGLE'S YORSH

<<<<<<<<<<<<<<<<<

Like all good quests, *Adventure* asks you one question: "When is a dragon a duck?" The answer is "When the dragon has to be rendered using 4 KB of cartridge space." The dragons of *Adventure* indeed have long, flat snoots that are reminiscent of a duck's bill. All the better to peck you to death with, my dear.

Word has it the youngest dragon, Yorgle, is as yellah as his scales. If you offer him a drink that flatters his color, maybe you can avoid a fight. If he chickens out and calls on his (equally silly-looking) brothers, fill the chalice that's bigger than you, chug its contents, and fare thee well.

FOR THE DRINK:
- 1.5 ounces citron vodka
- 2 ounces lemonade, chilled
- 0.75 ounce yellow chartreuse or other yellow herbal liqueur
- 2 to 4 drops citrus or spicy bitters
- 3 to 4 ounces blonde ale or lager, chilled

FOR THE GARNISH:
- Lemon twist or lemon wheel

DIRECTIONS:
1. In the serving glass, combine the vodka, lemonade, yellow chartreuse, and bitters.
2. Add standard ice to taste.
3. Add ale to fill.

CHAOTIC GOOD COCKTAILS

93	A Link Between Worlds
94	Baldur's Grape
97	BECAUSE I'M A POTATO
98	Door Hinge?
101	Elixir Syndrome
102	Fus Ro Dah (Into Oblivion)
105	The Ginger Catboy
106	The Never-Ending Ice-Cream Maze
109	The Plumbob
110	Portal Cake and Grief Counseling
113	Temple Rum
114	The Fighter, the Mage, and the Thief
117	Vanilla WOW!

A LINK BETWEEN WORLDS

>>>>>>>>>>>>>>>>>

SERVING VESSEL: Sling, collins, or other highball
SERVES: 1

The media is abuzz about multiverses thanks to a deluge of alternate realities from DC and Marvel. But Nintendo fans have been flitting through multiverses and across dimensions since Link took his first journey to Hyrule's Dark World in *A Link to the Past* for the SNES. The young adventurer has since traveled through light and dark in even measure, and he knows well that every mote of light that's in us casts a shadow behind it.

That's heavy stuff, but the iteration of Link that lives in *A Link Between Worlds* for the Nintendo 3DS takes the lesson to heart. His uncanny ability to become a drawing and shimmy through fissures quickly opens his mind, especially when he finds himself visiting a darkened Hyrule ravaged by monsters. If you're ready to accompany him, there's no shame in slamming back something sweet and strong. It might not open your mind, but it'll oil the gears a bit.

FOR THE DRINK:
- 0.5 ounce vodka
- 0.5 ounce white rum
- 0.5 ounce gin
- 0.5 ounce silver tequila
- 1 ounce melon liqueur
- 0.25 ounce lemon or lime juice
- 2 to 3 ounces clear cream soda

FOR THE GARNISH:
- Lemon peel

MODIFICATION:
- **The Hyrule Highroad (nonalcoholic):** Omit the vodka, rum, gin, tequila, and ice. Replace the melon liqueur with melon syrup and add a couple scoops of vanilla ice cream to the serving glass before adding the soda.

DIRECTIONS:
1. Optionally, use scissors or a sharp knife to cut the lemon peel into the shape of a Triforce.
2. Fill the serving glass two-thirds full with ice.
3. Add the vodka, rum, gin, tequila, melon liqueur, and lime juice.
4. Add the cream soda to fill.
5. Give the drink a quick stir.
6. Garnish with the Triforce lemon peel.

SERVING VESSEL:
Goblet or poco grande
SERVES: 1

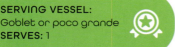

BALDUR'S GRAPE

<<<<<<<<<<<<<<<<<<

No matter how virtuously you intend to play your character in a tabletop RPG, something goes awry, and the next thing you know, you're in bed with five tieflings while a kobold tries to sell you a time-share in some dank castle. Sometimes you fancy yourself the dragonborn ranger equivalent of Saint Francis of Assisi, but your animal pals somehow all get rabies and bring down the curtains on the entire party.

The encounters in the *Baldur's Gate* games are necessarily a little more restrained; video game programming can't keep up with the screaming, chaotic depths of human depravity. (*Yet.*) Still, it's stunning how many unpredictable paths you can travel in *Baldur's Gate*. Every time you start anew, it really does feel like hitting the road again, your soul shining with good intentions that will inevitably land you on some level of the Nine Hells. Hot devil chicks, good drinks . . . eh, it's better than rotting in the shadow-cursed lands.

FOR THE DRINK:

- » 1.5 ounces vanilla vodka
- » 0.5 ounce grape schnapps or other grape liqueur
- » 0.5 ounce amaretto
- » 2 to 3 ounces concord grape juice
- » 0.5 ounce lime juice
- » ¼ teaspoon white edible luster dust (optional)
- » 2 to 3 ounces seltzer water, chilled

FOR THE GARNISH:

- » 2 to 4 green grapes, halved
- » 2 to 4 Moon Drop grapes or other dark grapes, halved

DIRECTIONS:

1. Put half the sliced grapes in the bottom of the serving cup.
2. In a cocktail shaker filled with ice, add the vodka, grape schnapps, amaretto, grape juice, lime juice, and luster dust (if using).
3. Shake for 10 to 15 seconds until well chilled.
4. Strain into a serving glass.
5. Fill the serving glass two-thirds full with ice, if desired.
6. Add the seltzer water to fill.
7. Garnish with the remaining grapes.

BECAUSE I'M A POTATO

>>>>>>>>>>>>>>>>>>

SERVING VESSEL: Martini, coupe, or cocktail glass
SERVES: 1

Oh. It's you. The years have piled on, but you've handled them well. I saw a gray hair, but that doesn't matter. You have so many hairs that *aren't* gray yet—even if your scalp is looking a little thinner since last time I saw you.

Never mind. We simply must catch up. Remember your dear little science project? The one your father clearly did for you, even though he's not your real father and therefore has no obligation to care? The science project about voltage that ended with me occupying a potato like a Dirt Ex Machina? It was very funny. Ha ha. It was so funny that I immediately taught myself how to manage my energy in crisis situations. Just in case someone ever comes along and decides to stuff me in a kumquat.

That means I had just enough energy to make you this drink. I think you'll love the arsenic—pardon, the vodka. I don't know how I mixed those up. Just drink, you rotten, terrible, horrible guest. I am TRYING to be a GOOD HOST.

FOR THE DRINK:
- 1.5 ounces potato (not grain) vodka
- 0.75 ounce coconut rum or other coconut liqueur
- 0.75 ounce horchata or other creamy cinnamon liqueur (such as RumChata)
- 1.5 ounces cream

FOR THE GARNISH:
- 1 teaspoon cream cheese, softened
- 1 teaspoon room-temperature butter
- 1 tablespoon powdered sugar
- 1 or 2 drops of vanilla and/or coconut extract (optional)
- 1 to 2 teaspoons cinnamon sugar
- 1 cocktail skewer

DIRECTIONS:
1. To make the potato garnish, in a small bowl, combine the cream cheese, softened butter, powdered sugar, and vanilla (if using). Use your hands to knead them together until all the sugar is incorporated and you can form a ball. Roll the ball in the cinnamon sugar and shape it into an oblong potato-ish shape. Set the potato candy aside in the freezer for approximately 10 to 15 minutes until firm enough to skewer.
2. In a cocktail shaker filled with ice, add the vodka, coconut rum, horchata, and cream.
3. Shake for 10 to 15 seconds until well chilled.
4. Strain into the serving glass.
5. Garnish with the skewered "potato" candy.

SERVING VESSEL:
Small goblet, coupe, or rocks
SERVES: 1

DOOR HINGE?

<<<<<<<<<<<<<<<<

There's lots of advice out there for those embarrassing moments when a band of "vicious" pirates clambers aboard your galleon and starts slacking and singing instead of actually doing helpful pirate stuff. Truthfully, there's only one solution to these discordant pests: Turn their rhymes back on them. Throw the word *orange* out there and watch them scramble for their footing like a landlubber trying to stay upright on a heaving ship sailing through stormy seas.

It's a little mean, though. Singing pirates don't cause any real harm to the ocean's ecosystem; they just want friends. At least treat them to some zesty grog before you say the magic word that will bolt their bearded mouths for good.

FOR THE DRINK:

- 1.5 ounces aged and/or spiced rum
- 0.75 ounce orange curaçao or other orange liqueur
- 2 ounces orange juice
- 0.5 ounce Falernum or Simple Syrup (page 8)
- 3 to 4 dashes orange bitters
- 2 to 3 dashes jerk bitters or other Caribbean spiced bitters (optional)
- Pinch ground allspice

FOR THE GARNISH:

- Orange twist

DIRECTIONS:

1. In a cocktail shaker filled with ice, add the rum, orange curaçao, orange juice, Falernum, orange bitters, jerk bitters (if using), and allspice.
2. Shake for 10 to 15 seconds until well chilled.
3. Strain into the serving glass.
4. Garnish with the orange twist.

ELIXIR SYNDROME

>>>>>>>>>>>>>>>>>>>

SERVING VESSEL: Glass bottle
SERVES: 1

Elixir-class potions are typically the most powerful restorative items in an RPG. They're always a welcome sight in the *Final Fantasy* universe, where they usually restore all your hit points *and* your magic points. A powerful restorative item like an Elixir doesn't simply grow on trees, of course. They come from clocks, at least in *Final Fantasy VI*. "So rare!" you say to yourself in a hushed voice. "I'd better save this until I *really* need it."

But that need never seems to swing around—or if it does, you dismiss it as "no big deal" that's nowhere near an Elixir-level emergency. As the game minutes pile up, so does your Elixir stock. Double digit stockpiles, triple digit stockpiles, gauntlets against enemies that rip off your skin and dress themselves in it while you lie dying—it doesn't matter. Those Elixirs are not to be touched until the need is truly there. It's like the digital equivalent of the nice dishes your parents keep aside for fancy company that never arrives.

FOR THE DRINK:

- 1.5 ounces pisco
- 0.75 ounce green chartreuse or another green herbal liqueur
- 0.75 ounce maraschino liqueur
- 0.75 ounce lime juice
- 2 or 3 dashes herbal bitters (optional)
- Pinch edible luster dust (optional)

FOR THE GARNISH:

- 1 small piece dry ice

DIRECTIONS:

1. In a cocktail shaker filled with ice, add the pisco, green chartreuse, maraschino liqueur, lime juice, bitters (if using), and luster dust (if using).
2. Shake for 10 to 15 seconds until well chilled.
3. Strain through a funnel into the glass bottle.
4. Use a pair of tongs or tweezers to add two or three small pieces of dry ice to the bottle.
5. For safety, drink only after the liquid has completely stopped bubbling and smoking.

SERVING VESSEL: Mugs or goblets
SERVES: 1 to 2

FUS RO DAH (INTO OBLIVION)

We dedicate this spicy-sweet mead to Lydia, the housecarl given to you by Jarl Balgruuf the Greater in thanks for shooing away the dragon that was harassing Whiterun. Lydia is your first companion, unless you play *Skyrim*, and she accompanies you when you climb the Throat of the World. She's present for the proud moment you learn your first Shout: the mighty "FUS ROH DAH!" She's with you when you begin your descent back to *Skyrim*'s sea level. And then, more often than not, she tragically disappears. She just vanishes.

There is no correlation between Lydia's disappearance, the narrow mountain cliffs, and the Dragonborn's itch to try out a new power that pushes things—and people—really far. Nope. Look it up, it's totally a glitch. Just pour one out for the vanishing housecarl next time you're slumming around the Throat of the World, and ignore any smashed bodies.

FOR THE DRINK:
- 2 cups mead
- ⅓ cup apple brandy
- 1 small green apple, sliced
- 1 small orange, sliced
- 2 cinnamon sticks
- ½ teaspoon whole cloves
- ½ teaspoon whole allspice
- ½-inch piece ginger
- 1 vanilla bean, split, or 1 teaspoon vanilla extract

FOR THE GARNISH:
- Apple and/or orange slices
- Cinnamon sticks

MODIFICATIONS:
- **Kaan Drem Ov (nonalcoholic):** Replace the mead and apple brandy with unfiltered apple juice or apple cider.

DIRECTIONS:
1. In a medium saucepan, combine the mead, apple brandy, green apple, orange, cinnamon sticks, cloves, allspice, ginger, and vanilla bean.
2. Cover and turn heat to low. Simmer on low for 15 to 25 minutes.
3. Remove the fruit and whole spices with a slotted spoon. Set aside the fruits and spices that you want to use for garnishing, discarding the rest. Alternatively, run the beverage through a fine-mesh strainer directly into the serving vessel(s).
4. Serve hot in mugs or goblets. Garnish with the fruits and spices you reserved earlier.

THE GINGER CATBOY

>>>>>>>>>>>>>>>>>>

SERVING VESSEL: Goblet, coupe, or wineglass
SERVES: 1

Final Fantasy XIV's G'raha Tia is a sharp-witted, resolute Miqo'te whose strength of heart and unwavering hope has carried his allies through more than one apocalypse. Yet despite all this strife, despite seeing entire worlds crushed by darkness and poisoned by holy light, G'raha is not world-weary. His distinctive ginger ears unfailingly perk up with joy when he's called to accompany the Warrior of Light on some adventure or another. He's playful, curious, and easy to feed.

G'raha Tia is an orange cat, in other words. And what better way to an orange cat's heart than a smooth, ruby-red strawberry cocktail made in the image of his widdle ears?

FOR THE DRINK:
- ⅓ cup apple brandy
- 1 small green apple, sliced
- 1 small orange, sliced
- 2 cinnamon sticks
- ½ teaspoon whole cloves
- ½ teaspoon whole allspice
- ½-inch piece ginger
- 1 vanilla bean, split, or 1 teaspoon vanilla extract

FOR THE GARNISH:
- 1 small strawberry, halved

DIRECTIONS:
1. In a cocktail shaker filled with ice, add the brandy, strawberry juice, ginger liqueur, lemon juice, and bitters.
2. Shake for 10 to 15 seconds until well chilled.
3. Strain into the serving glass.
4. Add ginger beer to fill.
5. Garnish with two strawberry halves inserted on the rim on either side of the serving glass so they resemble cat ears.

SERVING VESSEL:
Milkshake glass
SERVES: 1 to 2

THE NEVER-ENDING ICE-CREAM MAZE

Hey everybody! Why did the funny bear Muppet try to drown himself in a fifty-gallon ice-cream sundae? Because he BEAR-ly wanted to live when he learned he's in a game where he's forced to run dozens of ice-cream mazes while the same thirty-second loop of digital banjo diarrhea drills into his brain! Wakka-wakka!

No...? Okay, okay, here's another one. Why is the funny bear Muppet being forced to outrun monstrous dogs dressed like carnival barkers? Because there was a CLAWS in the contract he signed when he sold his soul to Muppet Satan for a new bow tie!

Hey, it turns out Hell has all the ice cream you can eat, but it all tastes like decomposing grandmothers! God is dead! Wakka-wakka!

FOR THE DRINK:

- 3 ounces vanilla whiskey or bourbon
- 2 ounces Irish cream liqueur or other cream liqueur
- ½ cup frozen blackberries and/or blueberries
- 2 teaspoons black (Dutch-processed) cocoa powder
- 3 or 4 dashes chocolate bitters (optional)
- 2 scoops vanilla or chocolate ice cream

FOR THE GARNISH:

- Whipped cream
- Luxardo cherry
- 1 black licorice candy cane or other black candy cane

DIRECTIONS:

1. Add all the drink ingredients to a blender.
2. Blend for 1 to 2 minutes until well-combined.
3. Pour into the serving glass.
4. Garnish with whipped cream, the cherry and the candy cane.

THE PLUMBOB

>>>>>>>>>>>>>>>>

SERVING VESSEL: Collins or other highball
SERVES: 1

If you didn't know, the little diamond (technically a hexagonal bipyramid, *harrumph*) that floats above a Sim's head in **The Sims** is called a plumbob. It displays a range of colors that change as things inevitably get more and more dire for your Sim.

You might see the deep green plumbob of contentment during the first few hours of the game, when you attempt to be a good shepherd to your Sims. That healthy green quickly fades to yellow when you give in to the urge to play **The Sims** like a jerk. Under your tender care, Sims pee their pants, get into fights, and flail helplessly in the pool after you remove the ladder. Before long, the plumbob blushes to a vivid crimson, confirming that your charge thinks you're Satan. Excellent job shredding that digital being's soul. Have a drink.

FOR THE DRINK:
- 6 to 8 mint leaves
- 2 slices lime
- 1 teaspoon light brown sugar
- 2 ounces umeshu (umeshu plum wine)
- 0.5 ounce lime juice
- 0.5 ounce Simple Syrup (page 8)
- 2 to 3 ounces brewed green tea, chilled
- 2 to 3 ounces club soda

FOR THE GARNISH:
- 1 lime slice, cut into two triangles
- 1 cocktail skewer
- Mint sprigs

DIRECTIONS:
1. Skewer the two triangular slices of lime with the bases facing each other so they make a diamond shape.
2. In the bottom of the serving glass, gently muddle the mint, lime slices, and brown sugar.
3. Add ice until the glass is two-thirds full.
4. Add the umeshu, lime juice, simple syrup, and green tea. Stir to mix.
5. Top with club soda to fill.
6. Garnish with the skewered lime.
7. Shpansa!

SERVING VESSEL:
Martini glass or coupe
SERVES: 1

PORTAL CAKE AND GRIEF COUNSELING

There are many celebrated things in this life that are actually lies. Truth. Justice. Mercy. Promises of cake after completing grueling trials. Promises that everything that troubles you in life, every cord of wood you carry, every splinter that digs into you, will vanish once you get grief counseling. All gone. A full belly, a clean mind, and topped-up insulin levels. That's what Aperture Science promises you, because it can get away with stringing you along before tossing you face-first into lies. And not even *normal* lies. We're talking about Whopper-size porkies delivered by a hanging computer homunculus that looks like the "Compliance!" alien from *Flight of the Navigator* got stuck halfway while trying to become a human woman.

Okay, so Aperture screwed you over. Join the line. Seriously, we've got a sweet and dreamy drink that's not actually cake, but it *tastes* like it, so that's something. We're fresh outta grief counseling, but we have some senior dogs you can pet.

FOR THE DRINK:

- 2 ounces cake-flavored vodka
- 0.5 ounce crème de cacao
- 0.5 ounce cherry liqueur
- 1 ounce heavy cream
- 1 to 2 dashes chocolate bitters (optional)
- 1 to 2 dashes cherry bitters (optional)

FOR THE GARNISH:

- 1 maraschino cherry
- 1 birthday candle
- Whipped cream
- Chocolate shavings or chocolate sprinkles

DIRECTIONS:

1. If you'd like, place the serving glass in the freezer for 10 to 15 minutes.
2. Stick the birthday candle in the cherry so it is fairly secure at the base of the candle.
3. In a cocktail shaker filled with ice, add the vodka, crème de cacao, cherry liqueur, heavy cream, chocolate bitters (if using), and cherry bitters (if using).
4. Shake for 10 to 15 seconds until well chilled.
5. Strain into the chilled serving glass.
6. Add whipped cream on top.
7. Place the cherry candle on top of the whipped cream.
8. Sprinkle with the chocolate shavings.
9. Light the candle. We are very, very happy for your success.

TEMPLE RUM

>>>>>>>>>>>>>>>>>>>

SERVING VESSEL:
Tiki or zombie
SERVES: 1

When smartphones started to become commonplace, the first thing we did was piss off a bunch of monkeys and start running for our lives through the South American jungle. *Forever*.

Auto-running games like **Temple Run** can be soothing to play. Hypnotic, even. You quickly forget you're running through a borderless nightmare jungle while dressed in the kind of Indiana Jones costume you see peddled at the grimiest level of social media platforms. Just pair that mellow high with a chilled pineapple-and-banana drink that has a bite of chocolate bitters. Be at peace and don't think too hard about how your immediate life choices are "Run to death" or "Get mauled by demon apes."

FOR THE DRINK:
- 1.5 ounces aged dark rum
- 0.75 ounce ancho chile liqueur
- 0.5 ounce mezcal
- 0.5 ounce banana liqueur
- 0.5 ounce falernum
- 0.5 ounce lime juice
- 3 ounces pineapple juice
- 3 or 4 dashes Aztec chocolate or mole bitters (optional)

FOR THE GARNISH:
- Pineapple leaves
- 1 to 2 pineapple slices
- 1 cocktail skewer

DIRECTIONS:
1. Using a sharp knife, cut the pineapple slices into small (approximately 1-inch) diamond shapes.
2. Skewer the pineapple diamonds on a cocktail skewer and set aside.
3. In a cocktail shaker filled with ice, add the dark rum, ancho chile liqueur, mezcal, banana liqueur, falernum, lime juice, pineapple juice, and chocolate bitters (if using).
4. Shake vigorously for 15 to 20 seconds until well chilled and slightly foamy.
5. Strain into the serving glass.
6. Garnish with skewered pineapple and pineapple leaves.
7. Add a few more dashes of chocolate bitters, if desired.

SERVING VESSEL: 3 shot glasses
SERVES: 1

THE FIGHTER, THE MAGE, AND THE THIEF

Fighter. Mage. Thief. Power. Wisdom. Speed. That's the sacred RPG class trifecta. Those are the jobs you reach for when you're serious about a quest. The Fighter hits hard. The Mage heals allies and/or attacks armored enemies. And the Thief dances like the wind while they relieve enemies of their possessions.

It's an effective combo—and maybe one that's too safe. Part of the fun of making your own RPG party is cooking up some zany class combinations that are guaranteed to make you suffer, because you hate yourself. RPG fans with *real* grit finish the original *Final Fantasy* with a party of four White Mages, and that includes the fight with Warmech. Nightmare incoming! Maybe some brightly colored drinks will stoke your courage.

FOR THE FIGHTER:

- » 0.25 ounce Grenadine (page 8)
- » 0.5 ounce honey whiskey
- » 0.5 ounce hazelnut liqueur
- » 0.25 ounce orange liqueur
- » 1 stemmed maraschino cherry

FOR THE MAGE:

- » Honey or corn syrup, for the rim
- » Popping candy, for the rim
- » 0.75 ounce peach schnapps
- » 0.25 ounce Blue Syrup (page 8)
- » 0.25 ounce amaretto liqueur
- » 0.25 ounce cran-raspberry juice
- » Pinch edible luster dust (optional)

FOR THE THIEF:

- » 0.75 ounce coffee liqueur
- » 0.5 ounce Goldschläger (or use any clear cinnamon liqueur and gold sprinkles)
- » 0.25 ounce black spiced rum

DIRECTIONS:

1. To make The Fighter, put the grenadine in a shot glass. In a cocktail shaker filled with ice, add the honey whiskey, hazelnut liqueur, and orange liqueur. Shake for 10 to 15 seconds until well chilled and strain into the shot glass. Garnish with a stemmed cherry.

2. Toss all the ice out of the cocktail shaker and rinse it, then add fresh ice.

3. To make The Mage, rim the glass with corn syrup and popping candy. In a cocktail shaker filled with ice, add the peach schnapps, blue curaçao, amaretto liqueur, cran-raspberry juice, and luster dust (if using). Shake for 10 to 15 seconds until well chilled. Strain into the popping candy–rimmed shot glass.

4. To make The Thief, pour the coffee liqueur into a shot glass. Hold a barspoon or other small spoon directly above the surface of the coffee liqueur and slowly pour the Goldschläger onto the spoon until it overflows and settles on top of the coffee liqueur. Using the same process with the barspoon, add the black spiced rum layer on top of the Goldschläger layer.

VANILLA WOW!

>>>>>>>>>>>>>>>>>>>

SERVING VESSEL: Rocks
SERVES: 1

Beloved online RPG *World of Warcraft* is over twenty years old. That's old enough to consider a serious career. And *World of Warcraft* has been growing and evolving alongside the people who've been playing it for decades. It's right there in the title: *World*. Life, even digital life, means dealing with change.

On the other hand, screw change. *World of Warcraft Classic* lets you play the game exactly how you remember playing it in 2004, when life was simple, and Shrek was pop culture's Messiah. Mix yourself an old-fashioned that delivers a velvety vanilla taste. Now imagine a tauren holding the drink in its big, meaty paw. *Aww.*

FOR THE DRINK:
- 0.25 ounce vanilla bean syrup
- 2 or 3 dashes vanilla or aromatic bitters
- 1 Luxardo or bourbon cherry
- 1 orange peel (optional)
- 2 ounces bourbon

FOR THE VANILLA BEAN SYRUP:
- 1 cup water
- 1 cup granulated sugar
- ½ cup dark brown sugar
- 1 vanilla bean, halved
- 1 to 2 teaspoons pure vanilla extract

FOR THE GARNISH:
- 1 vanilla bean pod
- 1 Luxardo or bourbon cherry

MODIFICATIONS:
- **Debuffed:** If you prefer a less booze-forward drink (but still alcoholic), make it a highball and add 3 to 4 ounces of chilled cola or cream soda after adding the bourbon. You'll need a taller glass, standard ice, and a straw.

DIRECTIONS:
1. First, make the syrup. In a medium saucepan, whisk together the water, granulated sugar, brown sugar, and vanilla bean. Bring to a boil over medium-high heat. Simmer for about 4 to 5 minutes until the sugar has completely dissolved. Remove from the heat and stir in the vanilla extract. Once the syrup has cooled, remove the vanilla bean halves and pour the syrup into a clean glass jar or bottle. Store in the refrigerator until ready to use. Save the split vanilla bean to use as the drink garnish, if desired.
2. To make the drink, in a serving glass, combine the vanilla bean syrup, bitters, cherry, and orange peel (if using). Gently muddle the cherry and orange peel. Stir to combine.
3. Add the bourbon and a large ice cube.
4. Garnish with the vanilla bean and another Luxardo cherry.
5. Sip slowly.

RATED M FOR MATURE

121	Better Days in Tahiti
122	The Sweat of Your Brow
125	Cordyceps
126	Cody Travers's Toilet Wine
129	Iced Hot Coffee
130	Itchy Tasty
133	Let's Go to Sleep!
134	Malenia, Blade of Tequila
137	P.T. (Potable Tea-ser)
138	Random Encounter
141	The Saucy Colossi
142	Seed of Hojo
145	The First-Person Shooter

BETTER DAYS IN TAHITI

>>>>>>>>>>>>>>>>>>

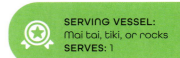

SERVING VESSEL:
Mai tai, tiki, or rocks
SERVES: 1

Red Dead Redemption 2 is a game about swell things that happen to swell fellows. An adopted family of outlaws grow close under the keen eye and wit of their patriarch, Dutch van der Linde. Dutch's amazingly executed plans bring in enough cash to fund the ragtag brood's early retirement to the warm sands and waters of Tahiti. There, the family toast Dutch with a spicy-smelling citrus rum drink of Hosea's own concoction.

Just joking. Wake up, Arthur Morgan. Things went terribly wrong at Saint Denis, you're freezing in a Grizzlies snowstorm, and you have to fetch John Marston because wolves chewed his damn fool face off. Good thing rum has a nice warming kick to it.

FOR THE DRINK:
- 1.5 ounces aged rum
- 0.75 ounce orange liqueur
- 0.5 ounce orgeat or 0.75 ounce amaretto
- 0.75 ounce lime juice
- 1 or 2 dashes sarsaparilla, sassafras, or root beer bitters (optional)
- 0.5 ounce corn whiskey or bourbon

FOR THE GARNISH:
- Cocktail umbrella
- Mint sprigs or edible tropical flower
- Grilled or charbroiled pineapple slice

DIRECTIONS:
1. In a cocktail shaker filled with ice, add the rum, orange liqueur, orgeat, lime juice, and bitters (if using).
2. Shake for 10 to 15 seconds until well chilled.
3. Strain into a serving glass.
4. Hold a spoon over the surface of the drink. Slowly pour the bourbon onto the spoon so that it overflows and settles on top of the drink.
5. Garnish with a cocktail umbrella, mint sprigs, and a grilled pineapple slice.

SERVING VESSEL:
Sour or rocks
SERVES: 1

THE SWEAT OF YOUR BROW

In 2007, a lot of us took a trip under da sea to a sunken fool's paradise called Rapture. As we descended into this watery hell, businessman and hyper-capitalist Andrew Ryan asked us a question: Are we not entitled to the sweat of our brow? *No*, Mr. Ryan scoffed. It goes to the man in Washington. It goes to the Church. In the Soviet Bloc, it goes to everyone.

To Mr. Ryan's credit, everyone living in Rapture put the sweat of their brow into making it a Gehenna of glass and steel. Not only are you entitled to your sweat down here—you're expected to drink it. No worries, it's fun to get trashed and make fun of the total tool who got those chain links tattooed on his wrists. Hey, Sweater Boy, 2001 called, it wants its visual metaphors back.

FOR THE DRINK:

- 1.5 ounces gin
- 0.75 ounce lemon juice
- 0.25 ounce Blue Syrup (page 8)
- 0.5 ounce Simple Syrup (page 8)
- 1 egg white or 3 tablespoons aquafaba, for foam (optional)
- Pinch fine sea salt

FOR THE "ADAM" INJECTION:

- 0.25 ounce Grenadine (page 8)
- 4 or 5 dashes aromatic bitters
- 1 small syringe

DIRECTIONS:

1. First, prepare the "ADAM" syringe. In a small bowl, stir together the grenadine and bitters. Fill the syringe with this mixture. Set this aside.
2. In a cocktail shaker, combine the gin, lemon juice, blue curaçao, simple syrup, egg white (if using), and sea salt.
3. Shake vigorously for 20 to 25 seconds until foamy.
4. Add ice to the cocktail shaker.
5. Shake for another 10 to 15 seconds until well chilled.
6. Strain into the serving glass.
7. Garnish with the syringe.
8. Inject the contents of the "ADAM" syringe into the drink before drinking.

CORDYCEPS

>>>>>>>>>>>>>>>>>>>>

SERVING VESSEL: Rocks, sour, coupe, or lowball
SERVES: 1

The *Last of Us* enjoys enormous popularity as both a video game franchise and a television show. It's also a cool teaching moment. Remember that beautiful, innocent moment in time when you didn't know about the cordyceps family of fungi that seizes insects' brains and turns them into spore-spewing zombies? Oh, sweet youth.

To be fair to the brain-melting mushrooms, they're just dishing back the trouble we give them. If living things can eat mushrooms—or drink them, in this instance—then they have the right to eat and drink *us* in turn. Anyway, don't panic just yet: Cordyceps fungi is highly specialized and only attacks members of the insect family. But who knows what this merry age of climate change will bring? Maybe ten years from now, we'll be petting giraffes in a lush city jungle. The last of us will be, anyway.

. . . .

FOR THE DRINK:
- 2 ounces mushroom-infused bourbon
- 1 ounce sweet vermouth
- 0.5 ounce walnut liqueur
- 2 or 3 drops walnut, celery, and/or aromatic bitters

FOR THE MUSHROOM-INFUSED BOURBON:
- 1 cup bourbon or rye whiskey
- 5 or 6 dried shiitake or porcini mushrooms

FOR THE GARNISH:
- Edible mushrooms, washed*
- 1 Luxardo or bourbon cherry

*Choose the most interesting-looking specimens available to you, such as chanterelles, oyster mushrooms, or enokis. Or, to make things easy, just use the dried mushrooms you soaked in the bourbon.

DIRECTIONS:
1. Put the dried mushrooms and bourbon in a mason jar. Let it infuse for at least 4 hours, or up to 2 days. Every once in a while, shake the jar to agitate. The longer you let it infuse, the stronger the mushroom flavor will be. So, if you are looking for a subtle umami afternote, infuse the bourbon for only 4 to 6 hours. If you want the mushroom flavor to really come through, let it go for the full 2 days.
2. In a mixing glass filled with ice, add the bourbon, vermouth, walnut liqueur, and bitters.
3. Stir for 30 to 40 seconds until well chilled.
4. Strain into the serving glass.
5. Add one large ice cube.
6. Garnish with edible mushrooms and a Luxardo cherry.

SERVING VESSEL:
Mason jar or plastic cup
SERVES: 1

CODY TRAVERS'S TOILET WINE

<<<<<<<<<<<<<<<<

Final Fight's Cody Travers is the quintessential example of the fallen hero who saved the city, saved the girl, but couldn't save himself. He cleaned up the streets of Metro City, only to become its biggest menace by starting fights for the adrenaline thrill.

Cody's brawls landed him in prison, where he found a twisted semblance of peace. It wasn't the Ritz, but prison was still a place to belong. Cody had a habit of busting himself out of confinement whenever he got bored, but he always came wandering back to his home behind bars. No surprise he turned his toilet into a vineyard. Booze is big business in prison, and who's going to tell Cody no? Not anyone who wants to keep all their teeth in their head.

Cody Travers is currently the mayor of Metro City. It's fine.

. . . .

FOR THE DRINK:

» 1 single-serve cherry mixed-fruit cup
» 1.5 ounces moonshine or vodka
» 1 to 2 ounces orange-pineapple juice, chilled
» 1 to 2 ounces unfiltered apple juice, chilled
» 0.5 ounce amaretto
» 0.25 ounce Grenadine (page 8)
» 2 to 3 ounces malt liquor

FOR THE GARNISH:

» Orange slices or wheels

DIRECTIONS:

1. Put the fruit cup (liquid and all) in the bottom of the serving vessel.
2. Add the vodka, orange-pineapple juice, apple juice, amaretto, and grenadine.
3. Add ice until the glass is two-thirds full, or to taste.
4. Top off with malt liquor to fill.
5. Give the drink a quick stir.
6. Garnish with orange slices.

ICED HOT COFFEE

>>>>>>>>>>>>>>>>>>>

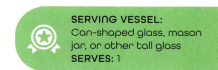

SERVING VESSEL: Can-shaped glass, mason jar, or other tall glass
SERVES: 1

The "Hot Coffee" scandal that lit up *Grand Theft Auto: San Andreas* like a percolator in 2004 threw one of America's biggest fears into focus: sex. It's not like anyone was thrilled that fourteen-year-old boys were playing a game about stealing cars from little old ladies, but that was apparently more acceptable than watching fully clothed game models made of five polygons each rub up against one another.

Never mind that this scandalous Easter egg was well hidden in the PC game's code, and never mind that it was about as titillating as watching some dumbass kid smash his sibling's Barbie dolls together. The United States was furious that their kids saw two characters making life together in a game that's supposed to be exclusively about blowing people's brains out. Sheesh, the world sure is a wild place. Why not come in for some nice iced hot coffee? It's ssspicy.

FOR THE DRINK:
- 1.5 ounces vanilla or whipped cream vodka
- 0.75 ounce ancho chile liqueur or hot cinnamon schnapps
- 0.5 ounce crème de cacao
- 2 to 4 dashes chocolate and/or coffee bitters (optional)
- 1 to 3 dashes spicy bitters (optional)
- 4 to 5 ounces iced or cold brew coffee

FOR THE WHIPPED CREAM:
- 1.5 ounces heavy cream
- 0.5 ounce Simple Syrup (page 8)

FOR THE GARNISH:
- Ground cinnamon
- Ground cayenne

DIRECTIONS:

1. Use a milk frother to whip the cream and simple syrup until soft peaks form. Alternatively, put the cream in a cocktail shaker and shake vigorously for 30 to 40 seconds until the cream is thick but pourable.
2. In a serving glass, combine the vodka, ancho chile liqueur, crème de cacao, chocolate bitters (if using), and spicy bitters (if using). Add ice if desired.
3. Top with the chilled coffee and give the drink a stir.
4. Spoon the whipped cream on top of the coffee and sprinkle with the cinnamon and cayenne.
5. Stir a bit to disperse the cream before drinking.

SERVING VESSEL:
Rocks or sour
SERVES: 1

ITCHY TASTY

<<<<<<<<<<<<<<<<

What did mom tell you about scratching your scabs? Stop it! They're just gonna get more infected—oh god, your skin is sloughing off. Okay, okay. There's a cure for this, right? This . . . skin thing? It's not like that guy outside bit you THAT hard. You won't wind up like the others. It's just—stop it! Stop *scratching*! Oh Lord, get that away from your mouth . . .

FOR THE DRINK:

- 1.5 ounces Itchy Tequila
- 1 ounce lemon juice
- 0.5 ounce Simple Syrup (page 8)
- 1 egg white or 3 tablespoons aquafaba, for foam (optional)
- 1.5 ounces red wine

FOR THE ITCHY TEQUILA:

- ½ cup tequila blanco
- 1 tablespoon szechuan peppercorns or 1 or 2 Buzz Buttons, lightly crushed

FOR THE GARNISH:

- 3 or 4 dashes aromatic bitters
- Dehydrated lemon slice

DIRECTIONS:

1. Put the szechuan peppercorns and tequila in a mason jar. Cover and shake to agitate. Let the peppercorns steep for 2 hours or up to overnight, agitating the glass every once in a while. Taste it after 2 hours to see if you'd like the tingling sensation and flavor to be stronger. The longer it steeps, the more intense the flavor and tingling sensation.
2. Once the tequila is infused, in a cocktail shaker, combine the tequila, lemon juice, simple syrup, and egg white (if using).
3. Shake vigorously for 25 to 30 seconds until very foamy.
4. Add standard ice to the shaker.
5. Shake for another 10 to 15 seconds until well chilled.
6. Strain into the serving glass.
7. Hold a spoon over the surface of the drink and against the inside of the glass. Slowly pour the wine onto the spoon so it overflows and the wine runs down the inner sides of the glass. The wine should settle between the foam layer and the bottom layer.
8. Add a few dashes of aromatic bitters on top of the drink. If you are artistically inclined, use a toothpick or stencil to create a design, such as the Umbrella Corp logo.

LET'S GO TO SLEEP!

>>>>>>>>>>>>>>>>>

SERVING VESSEL: Glass mug
SERVES: 1

Persona 5's Sojiro Sakura is a righteous dude in his own prickly way, but he admittedly sets up his troubled charge, Ren Amamiya, for failure. Sakura locks Amamiya in Café Leblanc every night and treats him with scorn during most of the boy's waking hours. It's no wonder Amamiya falls in with a bad crowd. The kid needs a friend, and it sure ain't his guardian for the first few hours of the game.

The closest thing to a real parent figure Amamiya has in ***Persona 5*** early going is Morgana, the tuxedo (NOT A) cat who's infamous for keeping his "master" safely contained in his dusty attic room. "Let's go to sleep," Morgana meows when Amamiya tries to descend the staircase that leads to the street. Morgana is just looking out for his roomie. Outside is trouble, and trouble will get Amamiya hauled back to the slammer. He's on probation, after all. Better to stay upstairs, have a drink, and maybe play some of those old video games he got from the pawn shop. Then Amamiya can curl up in bed and dream about the boot of society stomping on his face forever.

FOR THE DRINK:

- 4 to 5 ounces freshly brewed decaf (or not) coffee, very hot
- 1 ounce Japanese whiskey or scotch
- 0.75 ounce orange liqueur
- 0.5 ounce coffee liqueur
- 2 or 3 dashes coffee and/or orange bitters (optional)
- 1 to 2 ounces heavy cream

FOR THE GARNISH:

- Lemon twist or lemon peel

DIRECTIONS:

1. In a separate glass, use a milk frother to froth the cream until smooth and thickened but still pourable. Alternatively, put the cream in a cocktail shaker and shake for 25 to 35 seconds until cream is partially whipped but still pourable.
2. In a glass mug, combine the whiskey, orange liqueur, coffee liqueur, and coffee bitters (if using).
3. Add the hot coffee, leaving about an inch of room for the cream (or more if you'd like things extra creamy). Give the drink a stir.
4. Hold a spoon over the surface of the drink and slowly pour the cream onto the spoon so that it overflows and settles on top of the drink.
5. Garnish with a lemon twist.

SERVING VESSEL:
Margarita or rocks
SERVES: 1

MALENIA, BLADE OF TEQUILA

"I am Malenia, Blade of—" Yes yes, we heard you the first six thousand times you performed the Waterfowl Dance on our heads, *Malenia*. We get it. But we also understand how looking after a sibling can take a toll on a person, especially when you're swarming with a disease that's a stomach-turning combination of mange, syphilis, and scabies.

Good thing a stiff drink can carry anyone through the worst days in the Lands Between. Challenge yourself by drinking something so bloody and scabby-looking that the loathsome Dung Eater himself would put his hands on his hips and ask what your problem is.

FOR THE DRINK:

» 2 ounces tequila
» 1 ounce fresh blood orange juice or blood orange cordial
» 1 ounce blood orange liqueur or other orange liqueur
» 0.5 ounce lime juice
» 0.25 ounce Simple Syrup (page 8)
» 1 or 2 dashes orange bitters (optional)

FOR THE GARNISH:

» Chamoy, for the rim
» 1 blood orange wheel or dehydrated lemon wheel

MODIFICATIONS:

» **Scarlet Rot:** If blood oranges are not in season or available in your area, replace the blood orange juice with pomegranate juice or a cranberry juice blend (such as cran-pineapple or cran-raspberry).

DIRECTIONS:

1. Rim the serving glass with chamoy.
2. In a cocktail shaker filled with ice, add the tequila, blood orange juice, blood orange liqueur, lime juice, simple syrup, and bitters (if using).
3. Strain into the serving glass.
4. Garnish with a blood orange slice.

P.T. (POTABLE TEA-SER)

>>>>>>>>>>>>>>>>>>

SERVING VESSEL: Zombie or other highball
SERVES: 1

So many of us never left the house Hideo Kojima built in 2014. We're still in the company of the roaches that swarm the walls, and we listen to the shrieks of the best-unseen things that formed from our guilt-sodden memories. Once, we found comfort recalling the steady gaze Norman Reedus gave us after he shook off the house's veil and escaped. "I'll be back for you," his eyes promised. "Just hang in there." But it's been untold years, and the vision is fading along with our hope.

It's time to raid the hell house's liquor cache. Make a nice, bloody drink. Make it *salty*. Raise your glass to Lisa's restless spirit, but no matter what the radio tells you, *don't turn around*.

FOR THE DRINK:

- 2 ounces strongly brewed lapsang souchong tea, chilled
- 0.5 ounce Worcestershire sauce
- 2 ounces vodka
- 4 ounces tomato or vegetable juice
- 0.75 ounce lemon juice
- ¼ teaspoon celery salt
- ¼ teaspoon wasabi or prepared horseradish
- Few dashes hot sauce

FOR THE GARNISH:

- 1 to 3 mozzarella balls
- 1 or 2 small Spanish olives, sliced
- Few dashes hot sauce
- Lemon juice, for the rim
- Black salt, for the rim
- The saltiest pickles and/or olives you can find

DIRECTIONS:

1. To make the eyeball garnish, cut small holes in the mozzarella balls. Insert the Spanish olive slices into the holes until securely in place. Skewer the eyeballs on a cocktail skewer. Add a hot sauce to the eyeballs, if desired.
2. Rim the glass with lemon juice and black salt.
3. Pour the tea and Worcestershire sauce into the serving glass and stir. Fill the glass two-thirds full with standard ice.
4. In a cocktail shaker filled with ice, add the vodka, tomato juice, lemon juice, celery salt, wasabi (to taste), and hot sauce (to taste).
5. Shake for 10 to 15 seconds until well chilled.
6. Strain into the serving glass. Give the drink a quick stir.
7. Garnish with the eyeball skewer and any other pickled veggies you'd like.

SERVING VESSEL:
Hurricane
or poco grande
SERVES: 1

RANDOM ENCOUNTER

<<<<<<<<<<<<<<<

Random enemy encounters are a hallmark of classic console RPGs, and an unpopular one at that. If you're younger than thirty, you're probably not thrilled at the idea of walking a few steps on a 16-bit overworld, only to be accosted by the screen suddenly pixelating and whisking you into a whole new dimension of battle.

Mind you, a "random encounter" doesn't have to strictly be a battlefield thing. You know when your halfling cleric is at an inn and a half-ogre barmaid makes a pass at them? That's a random encounter. Or how about when a tiefling monk makes eyes at an elven druid across the butchered corpse of a kobold? A good shot of peach schnapps can make any random encounter seem like a destined one.

FOR THE DRINK:
- 0.5 ounce peach schnapps
- 2 ounces orange-pineapple juice
- 2 ounces base liquor (such as vodka, rum, gin, tequila, or bourbon)
- 1.5 ounces pomegranate or cherry juice
- 0.5 ounce raspberry liqueur

FOR THE GARNISH:
- Maraschino cherries
- Orange wheel

DIRECTIONS:
1. In the bottom of the serving glass, combine the peach schnapps and orange-pineapple juice.
2. Add ice until the glass is two-thirds full.
3. In a cocktail shaker filled with ice, add the base liquor, pomegranate juice, and raspberry liqueur.
4. Shake for 10 to 15 seconds until well chilled.
5. Strain into the serving glass.
6. Garnish with cherries and an orange wheel.

THE SAUCY COLOSSI

>>>>>>>>>>>>>>>>>>>

SERVING VESSEL: Zombie, tiki, sling, or other highball
SERVES: 1

Wander, the quiet protagonist of *Shadow of the Colossus*, starts his adventure with nothing but some simple weapons, his horse, and a determination that's as fierce as his grip. Wander latches on to his first assassination target, a monstrous stone minotaur that's bristling with grass, moss, and branches in all the right places for a nimble adventurer to make his ascent. Wander sinks his sword into the loamy spot atop the minotaur's skull, and the behemoth falls with a mighty rumble and boom. But that's just one Colossus, and legends say the others are so monstrously huge, the earth groans under them as they walk.

Wander needs a drink. Like, **really** needs one. If we were beside him in that chill, strange wasteland, we'd recommend something that's a little fizzy but packs a powerful rum punch. Maybe we'd garnish it with half a kiwi. Wander mostly eats cliff lizards; there's no way he's not hurting for vitamin C.

FOR THE DRINK:
- ½ kiwi, peeled
- 10 fresh mint leaves
- 1.5 ounces aged rum
- 0.5 ounce lime juice
- 0.5 ounce falernum or Simple Syrup (page 8)
- 2 to 3 ounces sparkling water
- 4 or 5 dashes black walnut bitters

FOR THE GARNISH:
- Mint sprigs
- ½ kiwi, unpeeled

DIRECTIONS:
1. In the serving glass, gently muddle the kiwi and mint.
2. Add the rum, lime juice, and falernum.
3. Add sparkling water to fill.
4. Use a swizzle stick or just give the drink a quick stir.
5. Add the black walnut bitters on top.
6. Garnish with mint sprigs and half an unpeeled kiwi.

SERVING VESSEL:
Collins or highball
SERVES: 1

SEED OF HOJO

<<<<<<<<<<<<<<<<

Genetics are interesting. Some of the most beautiful people in the world come from parents who look like a toddler sculpted their features before getting bored halfway. A key example is Sephiroth, the antagonist of *Final Fantasy VII* and indeed one of the most memorable villains of all time. He's a stunner with his cascading platinum hair, his confident grin, his mysterious, fox-like eyes . . .

Ahem. To get to the point, Sephiroth would have you think he's of divine making, and you'd be hard-pressed to argue against him. In truth, Sephiroth slithered from the same base origins as the rest of us. Not just that, but the man who contributed to half his biological makeup has the sloppy jowls of a hungry bulldog.

If you ever meet Sephiroth—the myth, the man, the legend—feel free to prepare this drink and deliver it alongside a lecture about where babies come from. Remind him that none of us actually came from angels, or aliens, or whatever silly idea he has in his head. Sephiroth will thank you for your honesty and absolutely will not skewer you like a shish kebab.

FOR THE DRINK:

- 2 ounces whipped cream vodka
- 0.75 ounce lemon juice
- 0.5 ounce orgeat
- 1 egg white or 3 tablespoons aquafaba, for foam (optional)
- 1 or 2 drops Saline (page 9)
- 1 or 2 drops orange bitters (optional)
- 2 to 3 ounces club soda

FOR THE GARNISH:

- 1 or 2 Luxardo or other cocktail cherries
- Cocktail skewer

DIRECTIONS:

1. In a cocktail shaker, combine the vodka, lemon juice, orgeat, egg white (if using), saline, and orange bitters (if using).
2. Dry shake for 20 to 30 seconds until foamy.
3. Fill the shaker with ice and shake for 10 to 15 seconds until well chilled.
4. Strain into the serving glass.
5. Top with soda water to fill.
6. Garnish with a skewered cocktail cherry.

THE FIRST-PERSON SHOOTER

>>>>>>>>>>>>>>>>>>>

SERVING VESSEL: Shot glass
SERVES: 1

Wolfenstein 3D. DOOM. Quake. Half-Life. Halo, Tom Clancy's Rainbow Six, and so very many more. If you were playing games around the time the first-person shooter genre began to gestate and evolve, you undoubtedly learned a lot about yourself as a gamer. You learned how to clamber up and around objects, how to take steady aim at an enemy, and how to pull the trigger faster than they did. Unfortunately, you also learned whether or not you are prone to motion sickness.

If you are indeed cursed with a shaky inner ear, don't sweat it. You can still take some shots with this sweet-and-salty drink. Better a shot down the esophagus than in the heart. Also, pro tip: Ginger helps settle unhappy stomachs. Keep a bottle of pickled ginger in your fridge!

FOR THE DRINK:
- 0.25 ounce mezcal
- 0.5 ounce orange liqueur
- 0.5 ounce hot cinnamon schnapps or hot cinnamon whiskey
- 0.25 ounce Grenadine (page 8)
- ½ teaspoon lime juice

FOR THE GARNISH:
- Honey or corn syrup, for the rim
- Black salt or smoked salt, for the rim

DIRECTIONS:
1. Rim the glass with honey and black salt.
2. In a cocktail shaker filled with ice, add the mezcal, orange liqueur, hot cinnamon schnapps, grenadine, and lime juice.
3. Shake for 10 to 15 seconds until well chilled.
4. Strain into the shot glass.
5. Take the shot!

CO-OP CONSUMABLES

149	A (Not So) Terrible Fate
150	Diplomatic Victory
153	Proto Man's Atomic Punch
154	Wine Flows Like a River
157	Wild Hunt

A (NOT SO) TERRIBLE FATE

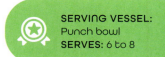

SERVING VESSEL: Punch bowl
SERVES: 6 to 8

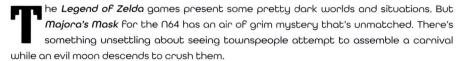

The *Legend of Zelda* games present some pretty dark worlds and situations. But *Majora's Mask* for the N64 has an air of grim mystery that's unmatched. There's something unsettling about seeing townspeople attempt to assemble a carnival while an evil moon descends to crush them.

Link advances the events of *Majora's Mask* before he plays the "Song of Time" and yeets himself back to the start of the three-day moonfall cycle. Imagine if the Hero of Time lost that ocarina and couldn't reset time. He'd be stuck, helpless to retreat. How chilling. May as well get wasted on the Happy Mask Salesman's private reserve.

FOR THE DRINK:
- 2 tablespoons fresh thyme (leaves only)
- ½ cup blueberries
- ½ cup water
- ½ cup blueberry jam
- 1 cup gin or vodka (use a blueberry flavored one, if you'd like)
- ½ cup elderflower liqueur
- 6 ounces frozen lemonade concentrate
- 2 ounces blueberry syrup or Blue Syrup (page 9)
- 1½ cups prosecco or champagne, chilled
- 24 to 32 ounces blueberry and/or acai seltzer water, chilled

FOR THE MOON:
- 1½ cups prosecco or champagne
- 1 teaspoon luster dust
- 4-inch (100-mm) silicone sphere mold*

FOR THE GARNISH:
- 1 or 2 lemons, sliced into wheels
- Blueberries and/or thyme sprigs

MODIFICATIONS:
- **For Deku Kids and Fairies (nonalcoholic):** Use ginger ale or lemon-lime soda instead of champagne. Omit the gin/vodka or use a gin or vodka substitute. Substitute elderflower cordial for the elderflower liqueur.

DIRECTIONS:
1. To make the ice moon, sprinkle the luster dust into the sphere mold, then pour in the champagne until the mold is almost full. Depending on the size of the sphere mold, you'll want to freeze for at least 6 hours or overnight.
2. In a blender, blend the thyme, blueberries, water, and jam until smooth.
3. Pour the contents of the blender through a fine-mesh strainer directly into the serving vessel.
4. Add the gin, elderflower liqueur, lemonade concentrate, blueberry syrup, prosecco, and seltzer water.
5. Add the ice moon.
6. Garnish the punch bowl and/or the individual servings with lemon wheels, blueberries, and/or thyme sprigs.

*These molds can be found online or in some craft or baking shops. They are primarily used for resin but can be used as ice molds. If you can't find them, there are smaller ice sphere molds widely available, which can also be filled with champagne and luster dust and used in individual guest's drink servings.

SERVING VESSEL:
Punch bowl, 1-gallon pitcher or drink dispenser
SERVES: 6 to 8

DIPLOMATIC VICTORY

<<<<<<<<<<<<<<<<

What kind of *Civilization* player are you? Do you conquer and colonize, or do you lay low and try to be friends with everyone? Even though it might be our rough human nature to fight with one another, we also have the capacity to forge long-lasting peace agreements that promise friendship and prosperity for decades. What's the secret? Economic stability? Nonaggression pacts? Yes, but also booze and caffeine. We humans might have a thirst for blood, but it turns out our thirst for mind-altering drinks is considerably stronger.

All bets are off if you look at Gandhi the wrong way, though. That dude will take any excuse to nuke you back to the Stone Age. But for everyone else, we've got some mead, some tea, and a chance to sing "Baba Yetu" as one race, the *human* race. Take that, "Kumbaya."

FOR THE DRINK:

» One 750-mL bottle mead, chilled
» 4 cups spiced black tea, chilled (such as chai or orange spiced)
» 1 cup peach or apricot brandy
» 0.5 ounce ginger liqueur or 1 to 2 tablespoons ginger paste
» 6 ounces frozen lemonade concentrate

FOR THE GARNISH:

» 1 lemon, sliced into wheels
» 1 orange, sliced into wheels
» Sliced fresh ginger

MODIFICATIONS:

» **Nuclear Ghandi:** Drop in the nuclear core (page 153).
» **Fog of War:** Use Earl Grey tea instead of spiced tea.

DIRECTIONS:

1. In the serving vessel, stir the mead, black tea, brandy, ginger liqueur, and lemonade concentrate until well combined.
2. Add ice to taste.
3. Garnish the serving vessel and individual serving glasses with citrus wheels and fresh ginger slices.

PROTO MAN'S ATOMIC PUNCH

>>>>>>>>>>>>>>>>>>>>

SERVING VESSEL: Punch bowl
SERVES: 8 to 10

Proto Man, the first-born robotic son of the genius scientist Dr. Light, is on the moody side. He's a lone wolf who roams wherever he pleases, though he never strays far from the side of his little brother, Mega Man. Proto Man has pulled Mega Man out of more than one jam, only to flit back to the shadows immediately after. Call it "Racer X" syndrome. Proto Man even has the shades to match the mystery.

But Proto Man is also a supreme introvert because his atomic core is just a touch unstable. If it detonates, anyone within Proto Man's orbit will be flash-fried, robot or otherwise. Better to just drift from place to place with the bottle at his side. Punch rides alone.

FOR THE DRINK:
- 12 ounces frozen mango, peaches, and/or pineapple
- Two 6-ounce jars stemless maraschino cherries with juice
- 1½ cups tequila
- 2 cups pineapple juice
- ½ cup orange liqueur
- ⅓ cup Grenadine (page 8)
- ¼ cup lime juice
- 24 to 32 ounces ginger ale

FOR THE NUCLEAR CORE:
- ¼ cup superfine sugar (or run granulated sugar in a dry blender for 30 to 60 seconds)
- ¼ cup confectioners' sugar
- 1 teaspoon baking soda
- ½ teaspoon citric acid
- 1 to 2 teaspoons spicy bitters or hot sauce

MODIFICATIONS:
- **Break Man's Batch (nonalcoholic):** Use a very spicy hot sauce instead of spicy bitters in the nuclear core. In the drink, omit the tequila and increase the ginger ale or swap it with ginger beer or a bolder ginger ale. Replace the orange liqueur with orange juice.

DIRECTIONS:
1. To make the nuclear core, in a small mixing bowl, combine the superfine sugar, confectioners' sugar, baking soda, and citric acid. Add 1 teaspoon of spicy bitters. With gloved hands, mix everything together until it resembles coarse crumbs. Try to smush the mixture together. If it doesn't hold or falls apart, mix in a few more dashes of bitters until it holds. Form the mixture into a tightly packed round ball. Set this aside for now.
2. In the serving vessel, combine the cherries (plus syrup) and the frozen mango.
3. Add the tequila, pineapple juice, orange liqueur, grenadine, and lime juice. Stir to combine.
4. Add a few cups of ice, or to taste.
5. Top off with ginger ale to taste.
6. Drop in the nuclear core. The punch will get progressively spicier as time goes by. You can remove the core at any time if you don't want the drink any spicier.

SERVING VESSEL:
1-gallon pitcher or drink dispenser
SERVES: 8 to 10

WINE FLOWS LIKE A RIVER
<<<<<<<<<<<<<<<<

Secret of Mana for the SNES is a classic action RPG that still retains a solid fanbase all these decades later. There's something about the entanglement of nature and budding technology that makes *Secret of Mana's* journey so unique yet so deeply relaxing. All those lush green environments are soul-soothing, especially the towering Mana Tree that lies at the bosom of all life.

Long, long ago, a greedy civilization used the power of Mana to make weapons, and the world was nearly destroyed in the process. Could such an apocalyptic event come around again? *Naaah,* people are great at learning lessons. Sit with your back to the Mana Tree, sip its holy nectar, and be at peace. (Until the Mana-starved Mana Beast reawakens in a rage and uses the planet for soccer practice again.)

FOR THE DRINK:
- 1 cup cubed honeydew melon
- 1 cup sliced green grapes
- 1 or 2 limes, sliced
- 1 or 2 kiwis, peeled and sliced
- 1 green apple, cored and sliced
- 2 bottles sweet white wine (such as moscato)
- ½ cup melon and/or green apple liqueur
- 24 to 32 ounces lemon lime soda, chilled

FOR THE GARNISH:
- Mint leaves

DIRECTIONS:
1. In the pitcher or drink dispenser, combine the melon, grapes, limes, kiwis, green apple, and white wine. (Use a smaller container if you don't have the fridge space.)
2. Refrigerate and let the fruit infuse the wine for at least 4 hours or overnight. If you used a smaller container for the infusion, transfer everything, including the fruit, to the serving vessel.
3. Add ice to taste, if desired.
4. Stir in the melon liqueur and top off with the soda to taste.

WILD HUNT

>>>>>>>>>>>>>>>>>>>

SERVING VESSEL: Punch bowl or pitcher
SERVES: 6 to 8

Imagine you're just a regular schmo going about your boring day when suddenly, boom—the Conjunction of the Spheres happens. The cataclysm turns everything upside down. Races and realms collide, and the world is full of faeries and monsters. Gnomes and humans living together! Mass hysteria!

And then there's the titular Wild Hunt, a group of specters that have a thing for running across the sky on demon steeds. Well, it's a nice change of pace from the apocalyptic horsemen that run the place on Wednesdays through Fridays. You can't sky-hunt, but you can witness the chase. Drinking and hunting go together like deer blinds and doe pee, so raise your glass.

FOR THE DRINK:
- 5 cups unfiltered apple juice or fresh apple cider, chilled
- 1 cup bison grass vodka or rye vodka
- ½ cup Krupnik spiced honey liqueur (or other honey liqueur)
- 1 cup brewed dandelion tea, chilled
- 2 cinnamon sticks

FOR THE GARNISH:
- Fresh herbs and/or whole spices
- Dandelions or other edible flowers, dried or fresh

DIRECTIONS:
1. In the serving vessel, stir together the apple juice, vodka, honey liqueur, dandelion tea, and cinnamon sticks.
2. Add ice to taste.
3. Garnish with herbs and dandelions.

MEASUREMENT CONVERSION CHARTS

VOLUME

U.S.	METRIC
1/5 teaspoon (tsp)	1 ml
1 teaspoon (tsp)	5 ml
1 tablespoon (tbsp)	15 ml
1 fluid ounce (fl. oz.)	30 ml
1/5 cup	50 ml
1/4 cup	60 ml
1/3 cup	80 ml
3.4 fluid ounces	100 ml
1/2 cup	120 ml
2/3 cup	160 ml
3/4 cup	180 ml
1 cup	240 ml
1 pint (2 cups)	480 ml
1 quart (4 cups)	.95 liter

WEIGHT

U.S.	METRIC
0.5 ounces (oz.)	14 grams
1 ounces (oz.)	28 grams
1/4 pound (lbs.)	113 grams
1/3 pound (lbs.)	151 grams
1/2 pound (lbs.)	227 grams
1 pound (lbs.)	454 grams

TEMPERATURES

FAHRENHEIT	CELSIUS
200°	93.3°
212°	100°
250°	120°
275°	135°
300°	150°
325°	165°
350°	177°
400°	205°
425°	220°
450°	233°
475°	245°
500°	260°

ABOUT THE AUTHORS

CASSANDRA REEDER launched her blog, The Geeky Chef, in 2008, bringing fictional food and drinks from a vast array of fandoms into reality with simple and fun recipes. Since then, a series of cookbooks based on the trailblazing blog have been published, including *The Geeky Chef Cookbook*, *The Geeky Bartender Drinks*, and *The Video Game Chef*. When not conjuring up recipes for fictional food, Cassandra can be found perusing the food carts in Portland, Oregon, with her husband and two tiny geeks.

NADIA E. OXFORD has been writing in, about, and for the games industry since 2004, which is the journalistic equivalent of being raised by wolves. She currently roams around in her half-feral state, consulting on games, localizing scripts, and publishing books to keep body and soul together. She knows a few things about mixing alcohol and video games, and guarantees these recipes are antifreeze-free. If words annoy you, Nadia also co-hosts the Axe of the Blood God RPG podcast and contributes to Retronauts' podcasts about old games and the weird pockets of culture they inspire.

PO Box 3088
San Rafael, CA 94912
www.insighteditions.com

Find us on Facebook: www.facebook.com/InsightEditions
Follow us on Instagram: @insighteditions

Published by Insight Editions, San Rafael, California, in 2025.

No part of this book may be reproduced in any form without written permission from the publisher.

ISBN: 979-8-88663-540-9

Publisher: Raoul Goff
SVP, Group Publisher: Vanessa Lopez
Publishing Director: Mike Degler
VP, Creative: Chrissy Kwasnik
VP, Manufacturing: Alix Nicholaeff
Art Director: Catherine San Juan
Junior Designer: Samuel Louie
Executive Editor: Jennifer Sims
Senior Editor: Eric Geron
Editorial Assistant: Jeff Chiarelli
Senior Production Editor: Nora Milman
Production Manager: Deena Hashem
Strategic Production Planner: Lina s Palma-Temena

Text by Cassandra Reeder and Nadia Oxford
Photography by Waterbury Publications, Inc.

Insight Editions, in association with Roots of Peace, will plant two trees for each tree used in the manufacturing of this book. Roots of Peace is an internationally renowned humanitarian organization dedicated to eradicating land mines worldwide and converting war-torn lands into productive farms and wildlife habitats. Roots of Peace will plant two million fruit and nut trees in Afghanistan and provide farmers there with the skills and support necessary for sustainable land use.

Manufactured in China by Insight Editions

10 9 8 7 6 5 4 3 2 1